Industrial Civility

Industrial Civility

The Primer of Politeness

by Alex M. Gow

Volume 4 in the Westphalia Press Civility Series

WESTPHALIA PRESS
An imprint of Policy Studies Organization

Westphalia Press
An imprint of Policy Studies Organization
1527 New Hampshire Ave., NW
Washington, D.C. 20036
dgutierrezs@ipsonet.org

ISBN-13: 978-1935907602
ISBN-10: 1935907603

Cover design by Taillefer Long at Illuminated Stories:
www.illuminatedstories.com

Updated material and comments on this edition
can be found at the Westphalia Press website:
www.westphaliapress.org

In Search of Civility

An archaic meaning of civility was 'study of the humanities,' and as a word it appears in the sixteenth century. The years have not blunted its importance; it is one of the guiding principles of *Wikipedia*, which informs readers that, "The civility policy is a standard of conduct that sets out how *Wikipedia* editors should interact. Stated simply, editors should always treat each other with consideration and respect. In order to keep the focus on improving the encyclopedia and to help maintain a pleasant editing environment, editors should behave politely, calmly and reasonably, even during heated debates."

Other voices also have been raised about the need to consider civility as a priority in an increasingly abrasive modern society. The Institute for Civility in Government in Houston, ably led by Cassandra Dahnke and Tomas Spath, has for many years hosted Washington seminars and blogs on the subject. Profesor J.M. Forni at Johns Hopkins has made a life's work out of studying the ramifications of civility. In the Hopkins alumni magazine he sums the current situation up when he writes:

We do have our manners. What we have lost are the manners of past generations. That we have manners, however, does not mean we ought to be perfectly happy with the manners we have. In fact, many Americans think that civility and manners are in decline, that this decline has increased in the past several years, and that there is a causal connection between incivility and violence. Does reality match the perception of a decline? Yes and no. There is little doubt that we are losing established forms of deference and respect. On the other hand, new forms of respect take the place of those becoming obsolete. A pregnant woman may not easily find a youngster willing to give her his seat on a bus. But the number of men willing to treat the same woman as an intellectual peer on the job is higher today than it was yesterday.

This does not mean that we should ignore the coarsening of social interaction that we have been witnessing in recent years. Our manners inevitably suffer when:

1. We are poorly trained in self-restraint.

2. We are used to seeing others as means to the satisfaction of our desires rather than ends in themselves.

3. We are overly concerned about financial gain and professional achievement.

4. We are constantly besieged by stress and fatigue.

5. We are surrounded by strangers who will remain strangers.

When some or all of these factors are at work, it becomes difficult to be considerate — and consideration is the ethical requirement of manners that are really good.

Clearly we need more people to take an interest in the topic rather than less. The Westphalia Press Civility Series demonstrates that the topic has many aspects, including etiquette and diplomacy. My friend Ambassador Mark Hambley suggests that there even might be some connection between the decline of cursive writing and the decline of civility. Unfortunately the current lack of civility in Washington is as noticeable or more noticeable than the state of the nation's handwriting. While politics has always been a competitive sport, common consensus is that the political life in the capital recently has become far more contentious than in recent memory.

The Westphalia Press Civility Series presents manners, etiquette, diplomacy, decent behavior, and politeness as fruit in the same orchard. The books are intended to be an accessible resource for studying facets of a subject that we think contributes to the current policy anxiety that has paralyzed decision making.

The subject has a universal aspect. Although we relish including George Washington as author of one of the titles in the collection, he actually found many of the maxims in his *Rules of Civility* in the literature of French Jesuits of the 1590s that was rendered in English by Francis Hawkins in London in 1640. By all account he was a man of manners no matter what the circumstances, and so we respectfully dedicate this series to his memory, in hopes that present day leaders will reflect on his example.

Paul Rich
President, Policy Studies Organization
Garfield House, Washington, D.C.

"SCHOLARSHIP WITHOUT GOOD BREEDING IS ONLY HALF
AN EDUCATION."

THE

PRIMER OF POLITENESS:

A HELP TO

SCHOOL AND HOME GOVERNMENT.

BY

ALEX. M. GOW, A.M.

PHILADELPHIA:
J. B. LIPPINCOTT COMPANY.

PREFACE.

HE is best taught who has learned the secret of self-control.

He is best governed who is self-governed.

Other things being equal, that school is the best where the government is the result of moral and not of physical force.

HINTS TO TEACHERS.

THE Primer of Politeness has been prepared to assist teachers and parents. It may be used as a text-book, or, preferably, as a class-book for study by the pupils.

All that is hinted at in this little book well-bred people know, but such knowledge is not intuitive, and it must be taught, if taught at all, to the majority of children at school.

The questions are numbered for facility of reference. Fifteen minutes a day spent in the discussion of the principles involved in this little book of illustrations will enlighten the minds, awaken the consciences, and control the actions of any ordinary children, and the few who are not governed by the instructions of the teacher will be controlled by the popular sentiment of the school.

The questions proposed are merely suggestive, but they by no means exhaust the subject. The habit of reading or hearing the illustrations read, and repeating their substance, is very valuable, not only as an intellectual exercise, but as a training in morals. The habit also of discussing the principles of moral obligation is invaluable. Hoping that the effort to help the teacher and the children in the government of the school will meet with approval, I subscribe myself their friend,

THE AUTHOR.

WASHINGTON, PENNSYLVANIA.
4

CONTENTS.

A*

THE PRIMER OF POLITENESS.

POLITENESS.

POLITENESS AND HAPPINESS.

DR. DODDRIDGE one day asked his little girl how it was that everybody loved her. "I do not know," said she, "unless it be that I love everybody."

1. How may we make ourselves and others happy?
By practising the *Golden Rule*.
2. What is the Golden Rule?
"Whatsoever ye would that men should do to you, do ye even so to them."
3. What is meant by politeness?
Politeness is another name for good manners.
4. Why should we learn politeness?
We should learn politeness in order to make ourselves and others happy.
5. How do you wish others to treat you?
6. Has any one a right to treat you ill or to make you unhappy?
7. Have you a right to make others unhappy?
8. Name something that another might do to make you unhappy.
9. Name something that you can do to make some one happy.

10. In what ways may persons receive harm from others?

We may be injured in our persons, our good name, or in our property.

11. How may your person be hurt?

12. State some hurt that might be done to your good name.

13. State some hurt that might be done to your property.

14. What would be the effect if everybody obeyed the Golden Rule?

True Politeness.

A gentleman in the West, while addressing a Sunday-school, noticed a little girl, shabbily dressed and barefooted, shrinking in a corner, her little sunburnt face buried in her hands, the tears trickling between her small brown fingers, and sobbing as if her heart would break. Soon, however, another little girl, about eleven years old, got up and went to her, and, taking her by the hand, led her toward a brook near by, seated her upon a log, and, kneeling beside her, took off her ragged sun-bonnet and, dipping her hand in the water, bathed her hot eyes and tear-stained face, and smoothed her tangled hair, talking in a cheery manner all the while. The little one brightened up, the tears all went, and smiles came creeping over her face instead. The gentleman stepping forward, said, "Is that your sister, my dear?"

"No, sir," answered the little girl; "I have no sister."

"Oh, one of the neighbor's children," replied the man. "A little schoolmate perhaps?"

"No, sir; she is a stranger to me. I do not know where she came from; I never saw her before."

"Then how came you to take her out and have such a care for her, if you do not know her?"

"Because she is a stranger, sir, and seemed all alone, with nobody to be kind to her."

15. Repeat the above story in your own language.
16. How does the Golden Rule teach politeness?
17. Why are some persons impolite?
Because they do not practise the Golden Rule.
18. How may persons be impolite to us?
By thinking ill of us, by speaking ill about us, and by doing unkind things to us.
19. How may we be impolite to others?
20. How may we make others respect and love us?
By thinking and acting kindly towards them.

Help Each Other.

An old Scotchman was taking his grist to the mill in sacks, thrown across the back of his horse, when the animal stumbled and the sacks fell to the ground. He had not strength to raise them, being an old man, but he saw a horseman coming and thought he would ask him for help. The horseman proved to be the nobleman who lived in the castle near by, and the farmer could not muster courage to ask such a favor of him. But the nobleman was a gentleman also, and not waiting to be asked, he quickly dismounted, and between them they lifted the sacks to the horse's back. The Scotchman lifted his Scotch bonnet, for he was a gentleman too, and said, "My lord, how shall I ever thank you for your kindness?"

"Very easily, John," said the nobleman. "Whenever you see another man in the same plight as you were in just now, help him, and that will be thanking me."

21. Repeat the above story in your own language.
B

22. When should we study to know and to practise the rules of politeness ?

We should study them at school and at home, and should practise them everywhere.

The Worth of Politeness.

Late one Saturday afternoon two ladies were returning home, when one of them lost a glove. Remembering that she had none suitable for church next day, she proposed turning into —— Street to buy a pair. According to the summer rule the stores closed early ; but one door was open, and that was of a small fancy and trimming store, which at any other time they would not have visited to buy gloves.

On entering, a modest young girl met them as she was passing out, and the proprietor stood ready to lock the door behind her. When asked, as a favor, to see their gloves, the young girl, though weary with standing all day, replied very politely, and showed as much patience and willingness to please as if it were in the early part of the day and she fresh for work, or as if the store had been her own.

The gloves were bought, and also some other little articles that lay in sight on the counter, and on receiving the money the young girl said " Thank you," as if the favor had been one done herself instead of her customers.

When the ladies left the store, one of them said to the other, " That is what I call true politeness ; now let's go there again when we are out shopping."

Neither had ever been in that little store before, but after that they went there whenever they wanted such goods. They were always met by the same polite and patient desire to please. They mentioned the place to their friends, and they know that they have added largely to the custom of that store.

23. Repeat the story of the polite young shopkeeper in your own language.

A Lesson to Learners.

When old Zachariah Fox, the great merchant of Liverpool, was asked by what means he managed to secure so large a fortune as he possessed, his reply was, " Friend, by one article alone, in which thou mayest deal too if thou pleasest, it is civility."

24. What is meant by civility?
It is only another word for politeness.

25. Is there any reason why we should be polite beside the desire to get rich?

The Boy and his Boat.

A young lad was rowing a gentleman across the Merrimac River. Some boatmen going down the river with lumber had drawn up their boat and anchored it at the place where the boy wished to land. " There!" he exclaimed, " those boatmen have left their boat right in my way."

" What did they do that for?" the gentleman inquired.

" On purpose to plague me; but I will cut it loose and let it go down the river. I'll have them know I can be as ugly as they can."

" But, my lad," said the gentleman, " you should not plague them because they plague you. Because they are ugly to you is no reason you should be to them. Besides, how do you know they did it just to worry you?"

" But they had no business to leave it there ; it is against the rules," said he.

" But," said the gentleman, " you have no right to send their boat adrift. Would it not be better to ask them to remove it?"

" They will not do it if I do ask them," he replied.

" Well, try it for once. Just run your boat a little above or below theirs and see if they will not favor you when they see you are disposed to be polite with them."

The boy did as he was told ; and when the men in the boat saw the little fellow quietly and pleasantly pulling at his oars to run his boat above, they took hold and helped him and gave him all the chance he wished. By being civil and polite himself the boy was unexpectedly treated with kindness and politeness.

26. Repeat the story of the Young Boatman.

27. Which acted with the more wisdom, the boy or the passenger in the boat ? Why ?

28. Does politeness ever require us to do wrong ?

29. May we say or do what is wrong to please anybody ?

Politeness only requires that we shall do right, as we would wish others to do right to us.

CONSCIENCE.

30. What is meant by conscience ?

It is that feeling of the mind which makes us happy when we do what we think is right, and unhappy when we do what we think is wrong.

31. Who are the happiest people ?

The happiest people are those who always try to do what they think is right.

32. Are all persons alike unhappy when they do wrong ?

No. All persons are not trained to know what is right and what is wrong.

A Troubled Conscience.

A lady about thirty-eight years of age, elegantly dressed, entered the shop of a gentleman in London in a state of great excitement, and asked if the owner of the shop were yet alive. On being told that he was living, she earnestly desired to see him. Being busy in watching the making of some candy, he asked to be excused, and called his daughter to wait upon her. The daughter went at once with her into the parlor. After sitting a short time the lady burst into tears. When she was able to speak she stated that more than twenty years before, she was a pupil at a boarding-school near by, which school this gentleman had for nearly forty years supplied with pastry from his bakery, and while there she had been in the habit of taking small articles from his tray, unknown to the persons who brought it. She had now been married some years and was the mother of six children, but still the memory of her thefts had so troubled her conscience that she was never happy. Her husband, observing her unhappiness, had after many trials got the secret of her trouble. He advised her to call on the baker and relieve her conscience by paying for the things she had taken, and also by making an apology for the wrong she had done.

The baker on being told the object of her visit begged her not to make herself unhappy any longer, as she was not the only one who had acted in that manner. After begging his pardon, which he most readily granted, she insisted on paying him some money which she thought was about the value of the things she had taken.

After remaining a short time she left, feeling that a great load had been taken off her conscience, and that hereafter she could be a happier woman.

B* 2

33. Tell the story of the Troubled Conscience.

34. What should we do when conscience tells us we have done wrong?

35. Why did this woman wish to ask pardon of the baker?

36. Why could she be happier after she had confessed her wrong?

The Window-Breaker's Conscience.

In the village of W., as a company of boys were about to go over to the academy, some one proposed to take the near way through an alley, and thus save some distance in the walk. It is not safe for boys to leave the open streets and to go through dirty alleys, for there are almost always some temptations in such out-of-the-way places as will lead them into trouble. On their way they had to pass a large warehouse that was used for storing wool. The side of the building near the alley contained several large windows. As the boys were sauntering along, one of them, who was generally their leader in mischief, suggested that it would be fine fun to break the glass out of the windows. Unfortunately for the owner of the house, there was not a boy in the crowd who had the courage to refuse to join in the mischief. There was no special reason why they should damage the man's property, as he was a kind, good man, who had done them no harm, but at it they went, and in a very short time scarcely a whole pane was left. After this exploit, which they called fun, they went on to school, seemingly highly pleased with their morning's work. It was supposed to be a good joke to destroy the property of a kind, good man who had given them no cause of offence.

One of the boys, who had joined the rest in breaking the glass, was ill at ease when he came to think of what he had done. He reasoned in this way: "Would I have broken the glass if it had been my father's warehouse? Would I have consented to see his property destroyed? Was it right to destroy property for fun? Was it doing as I would be done by? Was it brave or manly to sneak into an alley, in an out-of-the-way place, to do what I would not have dared to do if the owner had been present? To answer these questions in his own mind made him very unhappy. When he saw the owner of the warehouse he was uneasy and ashamed. If he were sent an errand and had to pass the gentleman's store, he would always cross the street. and pass by on the other side. This state of feeling lasted several months, so he determined to get rid of it.

It was nearly Christmas. He had been in the habit of saving his pennies and small silver coins to make some presents at the holidays. He had saved a nice little sum of money, when it occurred to him that the best use he could make of it would be to pay for the damage done at the warehouse and to get the owner to forgive him for the mischief. Accordingly, on New Year's morning he opened the box, put the money into a little red stocking, and, taking it with him, marched down to the gentleman's store. Walking in with a manly air and speaking to the owner, he said, " Mr. ——, some time ago, in company with some other boys, I broke the glass in the windows of your warehouse. I have been ashamed and unhappy about it, and as this is New Year's day, I want to begin the year right by paying for the broken glass."

" But," said the merchant, "you did not break all the glass?"

" No, sir," said the boy; " but I shall be glad to pay for it all."

The merchant refused to take the money, and, after a

few words of kind advice, he presented the stocking with its contents to the boy as a New Year's gift.

It required a good deal of courage and real manhood to act as he did, but the happiness derived from making an apology and offering payment for the damage was reward enough. The conscience, troubled so long, was now at ease, and its owner was a happy boy.

37. Tell the story of the Window-Breaker.
38. What did the boy do that was cowardly?
39. What did he do that was brave?
40. What is conscience?   See question No. 30:
41. What led the boy to offer to pay for the glass?
42. Was it right for him to offer to pay for the glass? Why?
43. Do persons always do what they know to be right?
44. How should we act with reference to conscience?

We should always obey the warnings of conscience, and do what we think is right.

HABITS.

45. What are meant by habits?

Habits are actions of the mind or body that have been learned by practice.

46. What kinds of habits are there?

There are good habits and bad habits.

47. What are good habits?

Good habits are such practices as tend to make ourselves and others happy.

48. What are bad habits?

The Weaver Boy's Habit of Study.

The late Dr. Livingstone was a cotton weaver, who worked from six in the morning till eight at night. He read many of the classic authors before he was sixteen years of age. His mother often had to take his book away from him to secure him proper sleep. When at his work he fixed his book on his spinning-jenny so that he could catch sentences as he passed to and fro, and the power of abstracting the mind from surrounding noises was thus formed. Thereby he was enabled during his many years of wandering in Africa to read and write undisturbed by the dancing and songs of his savage allies.

49. Tell the incident of Dr. Livingstone.
50. Name a good habit of the mind.
51. Name a bad habit of the mind.
52. Name a good habit of the body.
53. Name a bad habit of the body.
54. Name some good habit practised at school.
55. Name some bad habit practised at school.
56. Name some bad habit in the use of language.
57. How may we learn good habits?
By constantly trying to do right.
58. What is meant by character?
By character is meant the sum of a person's habits.

Good Habits make Good Character.

Amos Lawrence, the senior member of the long-known house of A. Lawrence & Co., was one of the most successful business men of Boston. He won success by his habits of industry and his business talent. His life is worth reading by every young person, as a help in the formation of his character. When a clerk in a store it was the habit of all the other clerks to mix a little liquor for drink and to enjoy a good cigar. Young Amos, though often tempted to imitate their example, resisted resolutely.

He said, " During the rest of my apprenticeship, five years, I never drank a spoonful, though I mixed gallons daily for my old master and his customers. I decided never to be a slave to tobacco in any form, though I loved the odor of it then, and even now have in my drawer a superior Havana cigar, given me not long since by a friend, but only to smell of. I never in my life smoked a cigar, never chewed but one quid, and that was before I was fifteen. I never took an ounce of snuff, though the scented rappee of forty years ago had great charms for me. Now, I say, to this simple fact of starting *just right* am I indebted, with God's blessing, on my labors for my present position."

59. State what helped to form Mr. Lawrence's character.
60. How may a bad character be formed?

Benedict Arnold's Boyhood.

Benedict Arnold was the only general in the American Revolution who disgraced his country. He had superior military talent, great energy, and remarkable courage. The capture of Burgoyne's army was due more to Arnold than to Gates. Had his character been équal to his talents he would have won a place beside Washington and Greene, inferior only to them in ability and achievements.

But he began life badly, and it is not surprising that he ended it in disgrace. When a boy he was detested for selfishness and cruelty. He took delight in torturing insects and birds, that he might watch their sufferings. He scattered pieces of glass and sharp tacks on the floor of the shop he tended, that the barefooted boys who visited it might have sore and bleeding feet. The selfish cruelty of boyhood grew stronger in manhood. It went with him into the army. He was hated by the soldiers and distrusted by the officers in spite of his bravery, and at last he became a traitor to his country.

61. Give the character of Benedict Arnold as a boy.

62. Why might we expect such a boy to become a bad man?

. 63. Why are habits so hard to change?

When we act from force of habit we often act without thinking. Sometimes the act is done before we think.

64. Give an example of a person's acting in school from the effect of habit.

65. May we excuse ourselves for a bad habit because it is a habit?

No. A bad action cannot be excused because it has been often repeated. We should change the habit.

Farragut's Change of Habit.

Admiral Farragut used to tell the following in relation to his early determination to be a sailor, and the reasons for it:

"Would you like to know how I was enabled to serve my country? It was all owing to a resolution I formed when I was ten years of age. My father was sent down to New Orleans with the little navy we then had to look after the treason of Aaron Burr. I accompanied him as cabin-boy. I had some qualities that I thought made a man of me. I could swear like an old sailor. I could drink as stiff a glass of grog as if I had sailed round Cape Horn, and could smoke like a locomotive. I was great at cards, and fond of gambling in every shape. At the close of the dinner one day my father turned everybody out of the cabin, locked the door, and said to me,—

"'David, what do you mean to be?'

"'I mean to follow the sea.'

"'Follow the sea! Yes, be a poor, miserable, drunken sailor before the mast, kicked and cuffed about the world, and die in some fever hospital in a foreign land.'

"'No,' I said; 'I'll tread the quarter-deck and command as you do.'

"'No, David; no boy ever trod the quarter-deck with such principles as you have and such habits as you exhibit. You'll have to change your whole course of life if you ever become a man.'

"My father left me and went on deck. I was stunned by the rebuke and overwhelmed with shame.

"A poor, miserable, drunken sailor before the mast, kicked and cuffed about the world, and to die in some fever hospital. That's my fate, is it? I'll change my life, and change it at once. I will never utter another oath, I will never drink another drop of intoxicating liquors, I will never gamble; and, as God is my witness, I have kept those three vows to this hour."

66. Tell the story of Farragut's reformation.
67. How may bad habits be changed?
By honestly, earnestly trying to change them.

A Battle with Habits of Appetite.

A gentleman formerly a tremendous whiskey-drinker, tobacco-chewer and smoker, but for several years past has been a reformed man, wrote to a friend in the city of New York as follows: "I have seen the time that my desire for tobacco was vastly stronger than it ever was for food. Once I was on a lee shore, the wind blew, the sea was tremendous. The last time I saw the rocky shore it was three miles to the leeward. It was late in the afternoon, I felt certain we should be on the rocks before morning if the wind continued. I felt in my pockets for some tobacco, but could find none. I examined every part of the vessel where I thought it possible to find any ; I inquired of the crew, but there was none on board. At that time I would have given fifty dollars for one quid. The gale ceased, we soon found a harbor, and the first thing I inquired for was tobacco. I chewed twenty-one years and smoked about eighteen. For a long time before I quit the use of tobacco I believed it was injurious to me, but I felt it was almost impossible to leave off. Eventually I was awakened and felt that such practices were sinful. I then thought I would try to leave them off. When I quit smoking I felt comparatively that I had lost all my friends. I could not eat or sleep as usual, I felt restless, and for some weeks thought it uncertain whether I should be able to conquer a habit which was so strong. But at last it was overcome. I then thought I would quit chewing, then came the struggle. To quit smoking was but a trifle in comparison. After I had determined to try to quit chewing, I always kept a piece of tobacco in my pocket; I was doubtful whether I should be able to leave off. Many times before I was aware of it I found I had had a piece in my mouth a long time. As soon as I perceived it I would take it out, but often before it was discharged I would give it one solid grind. There is nothing in the world, to me, so exquisitely sweet as tobacco. After several months the habit was overcome, but it was almost like plucking out my right eye. When I had entirely ceased from using it I had a better appetite, my sleep was sweeter and more refreshing, my mind more composed, my nerves were more steady, I grew more fleshy, and now I enjoy perfect health and can endure double the

c

fatigue that I could for a long time before I quit the use
of tobacco."

68. What is meant by Appetite?
It means a strong desire for food or drink.
69. How often and for how long must we try to change
bad habits?

The Uncontrolled Appetite.

The great temperance lecturer, Gough, told of a beautiful
girl in England, far gone with consumption, yet patiently
and lovingly toiling to support a brother who was addicted
to drinking habits. She used to get him a place to work,
but he would soon forfeit it by his evil ways, and so in her
weakness and pain she worked on, giving the renegade
brother most of her earnings. Little by little she saved a
small sum to pay the expense of her last sickness and burial,
which she expected would soon be upon her. The miserable brother found where she secreted her little treasure,
broke open the desk and robbed it, and spent the money
to gratify his terrible appetite for strong drink. To such
depths of meanness did he descend on account of his dreadful habits that even his conscience no longer troubled him.
Neither love nor shame could prevent the miserable man
from robbing his nearest and dearest friend.

70. Repeat the story of the uncontrolled appetite for
drink.
You need not answer the next two questions aloud.
71. Have you any habits at home or at school that you
ought to break off?
72. Are your habits of speech and behavior such as give
pleasure to all your friends?
73. If you have any bad habit, what should you do?

" I Can't."

The following sad confession of the despotism of an evil appetite and bad habit is narrated by a gentleman in New York, who heard the conversation.

Being in a coffee-saloon, a stranger stepped in one cold morning and called for a cup of coffee. The saloon had a liquor-bar attached, and the waiter, handing the coffee to the man, said, " Will you have anything else ?"

" Nothing else," was the reply ; " I drink nothing stronger than coffee."

While he was drinking the coffee, a well-dressed man whom he had observed walking the floor stepped up to him and said, with an earnest manner,—

" Sir, I would give all I am worth to be able to do what you are doing."

" How so ? What am I doing that you can't do ?"

" Why, sir," spoke the man, earnestly, " you can drink your coffee with a relish and refuse the liquor at that bar, that's what I can't do ; no, sir, *I can't do that.*"

74. Repeat the story of the man who said " I can't do that."

75. Why is it that people rarely reform their bad habits ? It is because they give up the struggle and say " I can't."

76. Is it manly or brave to say " I can't," and quit trying ?

" I'll Try, Sir."

During the war of 1812, between the British and Americans, an American army was sent into Canada. About sunset on the evening of the 25th of June, 1814, General Scott, with a party of twelve hundred men, came

up with the British army, which was advantageously posted
at the head of Lundy's Lane, near Niagara Falls. Although greatly outnumbered, the American general determined to hold his ground until the main body of the army
under General Brown should come to his assistance. He
opened the battle, but his small force was compelled to
sustain the full fire of the British infantry and of a battery
of seven pieces, consisting of 24-pounders and howitzers,
which crowned the heights, and at every discharge made
deep chasms in the American ranks. The evening was
now far advanced, and notwithstanding the moon was
shining in an unclouded sky, an almost complete darkness
covered the field, broken only by the flashes from the British guns and from the irregular discharges of musketry
on either side. A pause presently ensued as each army
prepared for a decisive blow, and the American general
gaining a partial view of the heights occupied by the British guns as the clouds of smoke rolled away from the field,
determined, as the only chance of winning the battle, to
make an attempt to capture the battery. Turning to Colonel
James Miller, who commanded the Twenty-first Regiment,
he asked him if he could take the battery. "I'll try, sir,"
was his prompt reply, and immediately placing himself at
the head of the attacking party, he commenced the ascent
of the hill. A sheet of flame burst from the battery,
carrying death and desolation to the devoted ranks. Closing up, they held their course courageously until within
musket-shot of the battery, when pouring in a volley and
charging with a shout, they bayoneted the artillerymen at
their guns, and, after a fierce struggle, drove the British in
confusion down the hill.

For his services on this occasion he was brevetted as a
brigadier-general, and he received from Congress a vote of
thanks and a gold medal.

77. Tell the story of Colonel Miller at Lundy's Lane.
78. Is it better to say " I can't" or " I'll try"?
79. Which is the grander thing, to overcome a bad habit or to take a battery?

The moral law says, " He that is slow to anger is better than the mighty; and he that ruleth his spirit, than he that taketh a city."

SOCIETY.

" *The New Commandment.*"

Archbishop Usher used to visit the clergy under his charge frequently and unexpectedly, to see how they were employed and how their churches prospered. On one occasion he went in disguise as a beggar to a clergyman's house. The clergyman was not at home, but his prudent wife scolded the unknown old man, though she gave him some food. "For shame, old man, that you should be a beggar. This is not the fruit of an honest, industrious, godly life. Tell me how many commandments are there?" The old man appeared confused, and stammered out " eleven." " I thought so," said she. " Go your way, old man, and take this book with you, and when next you are asked how many commandments there are, say ten."

The archbishop left, and the next day he had it announced that he should preach in the parish church. The morning came, and the good woman little thought that the archbishop was the beggar that she had lectured the day before until he gave as his text, " A new commandment I give unto you, that ye love one another." " It would seem by the text," he said, "that there are eleven commandments." The " old man" was at once discovered by the pastor's wife to be the beggar to whom she had given re-
c*

lief. She afterwards acknowledged with shame to herself
that there was another and a " new commandment."

80. Repeat the story of Archbishop Usher.

81. What is the " eleventh commandment"?

82. Why do people live together in society?

First, because they love each other's company.

Second, because they need each other's help.

83. In what ways do we need each other's help?

The strong should take care of the weak, the well should
take care of the sick. Some furnish food, some furnish
clothing, some houses, etc.

84. Name some of the classes upon which we depend
for food, for clothing, for medicine.

85. Name somebody that depends in some way upon
you.

86. Why are laws needed in society?

Laws are needed to protect the weak and to punish
those who do wrong.

87. Why should not every one do as he pleases?

THE MORAL LAW.

88. What is meant by a moral law?

A moral law is a rule which commands what is right
and forbids what is wrong.

89. What are the two great moral laws?

" Thou shalt love the Lord thy God with all thy heart,
and with all thy soul, and with all thy mind. This is the
first and great commandment, and the second is like unto
it, Thou shalt love thy neighbor as thyself."

90. What is meant by loving our neighbor as ourself?

It means that " Whatsoever ye would that men should
do to you, do ye even so unto them."

91. What is this rule called?

It is called the "Golden Rule."

92. Who is our neighbor?

Every human being is our neighbor, of every race and of every country.

93. How do you wish everybody to treat you? Why?

94. If you were to go to Ireland, to China, or to Africa, how would you wish to be treated?

95. If a Chinese boy, an Indian, or an African should enter your school, how would he wish to be treated?

96. How ought he to be treated? Why?

97. Does the color of the skin, or hair, or eyes make one person better or more deserving than another?

98. What is the effect of love toward our neighbor?

The moral law says, "Love worketh no ill to his neighbor."

99. What would be the result if every one obeyed that law?

An Englishman in Italy.

An Englishman travelling over Europe, when travellers were not so common as they are at present, on arriving at the city of Turin strolled out to see the city. He happened to meet a regiment of soldiers returning from parade, and, taking a position, waited to see it pass. A young captain, desirous of making a display before the stranger, missed his footing in crossing one of the gutters in the street, and in trying to save himself from falling lost his hat. The people standing by laughed and looked at the Englishman, expecting him to laugh also. On the contrary, he promptly stepped forward to where the hat lay, and, taking it up, presented it with an air of kindness to its confused owner. The officer took it with a blush of surprise and pleasure, and hurried to rejoin his company. There was a murmur of applause, and the stranger passed on. Not a word was spoken, but every one who witnessed the scene was pleased with the politeness of the stranger.

After the regiment was dismissed the captain told his story to his colonel ; the colonel immediately mentioned it to the general in command, and when the Englishman returned to his hotel, he found an officer waiting to request his company to dinner at the headquarters. In the evening he was taken to the palace of the king, and was received with particular attention. Of course, during his stay in Turin he was invited everywhere, and on his departure was given letters of introduction to prominent citizens of the different cities of Italy. Thus a private gentleman of moderate means was enabled to travel under the most favorable circumstances, to visit the most celebrated cities and to meet the best society, because he had taken the opportunity of doing a kindness to a stranger. Acts of kindness rarely fail to make warm friends.

100. Give the story of the Englishman's politeness.

101. Does the Golden Rule mean that we shall treat all persons alike?

No. It means that we should treat every person as we would like to be treated if we were in his place and he in ours.

SOCIAL GRADES.

102. What classes of persons in society require different treatment from us?

Our Superiors, our Equals, and our Inferiors.

103. Who are the *Superiors* of boys and girls?

Their parents, their teachers, and those who are older and wiser than they.

104. Who are the *Equals* of boys and girls?

Their class-mates, school-mates, brothers and sisters, and others of about the same age.

105. Who are the *Inferiors* of boys and girls?

Those who are younger and weaker, or those who are more ignorant.

HONOR TO PARENTS.

Washington's Regard for his Mother.

General Washington, when quite young, was about to go to sea as a midshipman. Everything was arranged, the vessel lay opposite his father's house, the little boat had come on shore to take him off, and his whole heart was bent on going. After his trunk had been carried down to the boat he went to bid his mother farewell, and saw the tears bursting from her eyes. He said nothing to her, but seeing she would be distressed if he went, and perhaps would never be happy again, he turned to the servant and said, " Go tell them to take my trunk back ; I will not go away to break my mother's heart." His mother was struck with his decision, and said to him, " George, God has promised to bless the children that honor their parents, and I believe he will bless you."

106. Relate the story of Washington's regard for his mother.

107. How should children treat their parents?

The moral law says, " Honor thy father and mother."

108. Why should children obey their parents?

A Wise Mother and a Dutiful Son.

The Hon. Thomas H. Benton paid the following beautiful tribute to his mother. He said, " My mother asked me never to use tobacco. I never touched it from that day to this. She asked me never to gamble, and I have never gambled ; I cannot tell who is losing in games that are being played. She admonished me, too, against hard drinking, and whatever capacity for endurance I have at present, and whatever usefulness I have, I attribute to having complied with her pious and correct wishes. When I was seven years of age she asked me not to drink, and I then made a resolution of total abstinence ; and that I have adhered to it through all time, I owe to my mother."

109. Tell the story of Mrs. Benton and her son.
110. In what respect are your parents your superiors ?

Hurting his Father.

A boy was tempted by some of his companions to take some fruit from a tree which his father had forbidden him to touch.

" You need not be afraid," said they, " for if your father should find out that you had taken them, he is so kind that he will not hurt you."

" That is the very reason," replied the boy, " why I should not touch the apples. My father may not hurt me, yet I know my disobedience would hurt him, and that would be worse to me than anything else."

111. Repeat the story of the boy's hurting his father.
112. How should children fear their parents ?
They should fear to displease them by disobedience.
113. How should children speak and act towards their parents ?
114. How should children speak about their parents ?
115. How should parents treat disobedient children ?

HONOR TO TEACHERS.

116. How is the teacher superior to children?

In age, in learning, and in wisdom.

117. What are the reasons why children should obey their teacher?

1st. Because obedience to our parents requires obedience to the teacher.

2d. Because the teacher will love us if we are kind and obedient.

3d. The good of the school requires that all shall obey the teacher's rules.

118. How may a teacher be compelled to love the children?

119. How should children speak and act to their teacher?

120. How should children always speak of their teacher?

121. Why are children often so unhappy at school? Is it because they are always kind, polite, obliging, and obedient?

Bad Company and Bad Advice.

Judge Buller, when in the company of a young man of sixteen, cautioned him against being led astray by the example or persuasion of others, and said, "If I had listened to the advice of some of those who called themselves my friends when I was young, instead of being a judge of the King's Bench I should have died long ago a prisoner of the King's Bench."

122. Repeat Judge Buller's caution.

123. Why do children disobey the rules of school?

1st. For want of respect for themselves.

2d. For want of regard for their parents and teacher.

3d. On account of bad advice from others.

124. What should be done with those who disobey the laws of school?

HONOR TO THE AGED.

"*Somebody's Mother.*"

The conductor on the cars which reached Clinton, Indiana, from the West was so kind to an old lady when she got off the train at De Witt, and he rendered her so much assistance in getting her baggage to the depot, that a passenger asked him if the old lady was his mother. "Oh, no," was the reply, "but she is somebody's mother." This is the conduct of a true gentleman, and is in strange contrast with that of those who do not understand that true politeness consists in a kind and respectful attention to the wants and wishes of the aged. The moral law says, "Thou shalt rise up before the hoary head, and honor the face of the old man, and fear thy God."

125. Repeat the story of the polite conductor and somebody's mother.

126. What is meant by "the hoary head"?

127. How would you wish your father and mother to be treated?

How School-boys Preached a Sermon.

A sermon can be preached by acts as well as by words. The boys of a New York school, some time since, preached one on charity. An old widow of about seventy years had for seven years past a candy and cake stand in front of the school building. She was very popular with the boys, and by their patronage supported herself and an invalid son.

Certain storekeepers in the neighborhood sought to drive the old lady away, as her little trade interfered with their business. By some one her stand was knocked over, and her stock of candies—scarcely worth two dollars—was broken into small pieces. The boys, coming out of school and seeing her distress, devoted their pennies to her relief, each one taking a fragment and paying the price of the whole piece, until she had received twelve dollars.

But they did not stop at that part of the sermon. Two tons of coal, a bountiful supply of provisions, and a receipt for two months' rent were sent to her by the boy preachers. Then they went to the board of education and so represented her case that the old lady received official permission to occupy her usual place in front of the school building. Respect for the aged is one of the most beautiful traits of youth.

128. Repeat the story of the New York school-boys.

129. How may we show our respect for the aged ?

1st. By offering to help them when they need help.

2d. By respecting their feelings.

3d. By obeying their wishes.

4th. By listening respectfully to their advice.

130. How should children speak to their elders ?

131. How should children speak of their elders ?

132. Why should young people listen to the advice of their superiors ?

1st. Because age and experience have given them wisdom.

2d. Because they are our friends, who wish us well.

POLITENESS TO SUPERIORS.

An Elderly Customer.

Kind hearts are sure to show themselves in kind actions, and young people ought always to be thoughtful and attentive to the aged. Courtesy to others is often one of the

D

most effective ways of getting on in the world. An incident in proof of this.

There was a very plainly dressed, elderly lady, who was
a frequent customer at the then leading dry-goods store in
Boston. No one in the store knew her, even by name. All
the clerks but one avoided her, and gave their attentions to
those who were better dressed and more pretentious. The
exception was one young man, who had a conscientious regard for duty and system. He never left another customer
to wait on the lady, but when at liberty, he waited upon
her with as much attention as though she had been a princess. This continued for a year or two, until the young
man became of age. One morning the lady approached
the young man, when the following conversation took place :
"Young man, do you want to go into business for yourself?"

"Yes, ma'am," he responded ; "but I have neither
money, credit, nor friends, nor will any one trust me."

"Well," continued the lady, "you go and select a good
location, ask what the rent is, and report to me," handing
the young man her address.

The young man went, found a capital location and good
store, but the landlord required security, which he could
not give. Mindful of the lady's request, he forthwith went
to her and reported.

"Well," she replied, "you go and tell Mr. —— that I
will be responsible."

He went, and the landlord, or agent, was surprised, but
the bargain was closed. The next day the lady called to
ascertain the result. The young man told her, but added,
"What am I to do for goods? No one will trust me."

"You may go and see Mr. ——, and Mr. ——, and Mr.
——, and tell them to call on me."

He did, and his store was soon stocked with the best goods

in the market. There are many in this city who remember the circumstances and the man, says a Boston paper. He died many years since, and left a fortune of three hundred thousand dollars. So much for politeness, and so much for civility, and so much for treating one's elders with the deference due to age, in whatever garb they are clothed.

133. Repeat the story of the polite clerk.
134. Shall we be polite only for the sake of benefits? Repeat the Golden Rule. See No. 91.

POLITENESS TO EQUALS.

BROTHERS AND SISTERS.

135. In what way should the children of the family be equal?

They are equal, according to their age, in all the rights and privileges of home.

136. In what are they unequal?

They may be unequal in age, in knowledge, and in bodily strength.

137. How should the stronger use their strength?

1st. In defending the weaker ones.

2d. In helping those that need help.

3d. In teaching kindness and politeness.

138. How shall the younger and weaker treat those who are older?

1st. They should return kindness for kindness.

2d. They should give no more trouble than is necessary.

3d. They should be willing to be taught.

139. How should each child in the family act toward the rest?

Every one should practise the Golden Rule.

140. When children are selfish, cross, or mischievous, what is the effect on the rest of the family?

141. Upon what does the happiness of the home largely depend?

The Young Nurse.

Voluntary suffering for the good of others is always noble, but when this is multiplied and embittered by one's own recent affliction, the effort is truly heroic. The *Presbyterian* of Memphis thus refers to an incident of the late yellow fever plague in that city:

" The following is but one of many scenes of sorrow and self-sacrifice which have been witnessed in our city. It was in a family of six,—a father and mother, two sisters, and two brothers. The fever entered their house, and all were stricken down but one little boy of twelve years. He alone was left to minister to them.

"The mother was called away, and the little boy was well-nigh broken-hearted. The physician had just called when the mother died, and turning to the weeping child, said to him,—

" 'You must dry up your tears and go wait upon your sisters, and don't let them know, by your crying, that your ma is dead, for it may hurt them.'

" Brave little fellow ! He went instantly, washed his face and dried his tears, and entered the room where his sick sisters lay. The first question which was asked him was, ' How is ma ?'

" No tears betrayed the heavy heart, but choking down his sorrow, with cheerful tone he answered, ' Ma is better off now,' and the sisters did not know their loss. Surely there is other heroism than that which is on battle-fields."

142. Repeat the story of the boy nurse.

143. How should the sick or the infirm act toward the rest of the family?

1st. They should not be fretful or fault-finding.

2d. They should be as patient as possible.

3d. They should give as little trouble as possible.

4th. They should never forget to be polite to those who care for them.

The two following questions need not be answered aloud:

144. Is your home as happy as it might be?

145. Do you do all you can to make your home happy?

SCHOOL-MATES AS EQUALS.

146. In what respect should school-mates be considered equal?

They should be equal in all the rights and privileges ot the school.

147. How are school-mates unequal?

They are unequal in age, in size, in strength, and in learning.

148. How should the older, larger, and stronger children treat the rest?

Losing a Button.

Walter Scott tells a story of a boy who was with him in school, who always stood at the head of his class. It was the custom of the scholars to change places in their classes according to failure or success in recitation; but though Walter was number two, he could not get to the head, because this boy never missed. But Walter noticed that he had a habit, when puzzled by a hard question, of twirling a button on his jacket, and this seemed to help him think out a right answer.

Walter, more through mischief than any worse motive, cut off the button slyly one day, to see if it would make

D*

any difference. The lesson was a spelling lesson, and several boys at the foot missed a hard word. It came round to the head. The boy instinctively put his hand to the button. It was gone. He looked down to find it, grew confused, missed the word, and Walter went above him. The boy never got to the head again, seemed to lose his ambition, settled down into a second-rate scholar, and never accomplished much in life. Walter Scott declared that he often suffered sharp remorse at the thought that he possibly spoiled the boy for school and for life by cutting off the button that had done such good service.

149. Repeat the story of Walter Scott.

150. Was it right to take advantage of a class-mate in that way? Why?

151. Has each one a right to excel in scholarship? Why?

152. Has each a right to excel in politeness? Why?

153. Should there be any difference in the treatment of children in school on account of the wealth or social standing of their parents?

154. Should there be any difference in the treatment of children in school on account of race or color? Why?

155. Because we treat everybody politely must we make bosom friends of every one?

We should be polite to everybody, but only intimate with a few.

POLITENESS TO INFERIORS.

156. Who are the inferiors of boys and girls?

Those who are younger or weaker or more ignorant than they.

157. How should we treat those whom we think are our inferiors?

We should treat them as we would wish our superiors to treat us.

Assumed Superiority, a Fable.

A humming-bird met a butterfly, and, being pleased with the beauty of its person and the glory of its wings, made an offer of perpetual friendship.

" I cannot think of it," was the reply, "as you once spurned me and called me a crawling dolt."

" Impossible !" exclaimed the humming-bird. " I always entertained the highest respect for such creatures as you."

" Perhaps you do now," said the other ; " but when you insulted me I was a caterpillar. So let me give you a bit of advice : Never insult the humble, as they may some day become your superiors."

158. Repeat the fable and state its moral.

159. If we refuse to be polite to others what may we expect to receive from them ?

" In Honor preferring One Another."

This is a sermon,—a kind of sermon, at any rate,—and of course it must have a text, and the text of this sermon is the verse, or, rather, the part of the verse, placed at the head of it. This sermon will have three parts,—an explanation, an illustration, and an application.

1st. *The Explanation.*—The explanation is to be an explanation of the text. The text means that in our dealings with our fellow-creatures we must treat everybody with kind and respectful consideration.

The whole verse is this, " Be kindly affectioned one to another in brotherly love ; in honor preferring one another." The word honor means respectful politeness, and the precept therefore means that in our dealings with our fellow-creat-

ures we must treat everybody in a respectful and proper
manner. *Everybody.* It does not say in honor preferring
the rich and the great, but *one another*,—that is, everybody
that we have anything to do with. So much for the explanation of the text. Now for the illustration of the meaning of it.

2d. *The Illustration.*—A poor old woman was engaged
one morning mopping down the stairs at a hotel. Before
she had finished the work some gentlemen began to come
in,—travellers who had arrived by an early train.

The first that came was a man they called colonel. He
was not a real colonel, but only a make-believe. He came
hurrying along, and without giving the poor woman time
to move her pail said to her, in a rude and surly voice,
"Take your pail out of the way, old woman. Can't
you get your work done up in the morning earlier than
this?"

He looked upon the woman with an expression of contempt upon his countenance as he passed her, and muttered
to another man who was behind him as he went up the
stairs, "What an ugly old hag!"

Very soon afterwards two other gentlemen came in. The
foremost, who was somewhat advanced in life, had a travel-
ling-bag in his hand. The other one, who was younger,
followed him. The old gentleman paused a moment as he
came up, and then said, "Don't move your pail, ma'am;
I can step over it." She, however, made haste to move it.
"I am sorry to disturb you at your work," said he, and
looked down at her with a smile and nodded as he passed.
The poor woman's face was lighted up with something like
a smile in return, and as the gentleman passed on she said
to herself,—

"There's one man, at least, that don't hate me." And a
tear came into her eye.

When the two gentlemen reached the top of the stairs the younger one said to the older, in a joking way,—

" You were very polite to the old woman, brother George."

" Well," rejoined George, " stop a minute and look at her."

They had by this time reached the top of the stairs, and had begun to turn to go along the hall, but they stopped and looked over the baluster at the woman, still going on with her work below.

" Look at her," said the old gentleman, speaking, however, in a low tone, so that the woman did not hear him. She did not even notice that the gentlemen had stopped. " Look at her. See her sallow and wrinkled face; and what a care-worn and sorrowful expression upon it! There was a time when she was a young girl, with a blooming face and white neck, and young men in love with her. Everything in life looked bright and happy to her then. But look at her now. Poor thing! We can't help her much, but we can at any rate respect her misfortunes, and speak a kind word to her as we go by."

3d. And now for *the application.* Whenever you see a poor woman, or a poor man, or even a poor child in the street, do not treat them in a harsh and contemptuous manner, but speak to them, if you have occasion to speak at all, in a kind and considerate tone. By so doing you will be obeying the precept of the text, and instead of adding to the humiliation and suffering of the poor and the miserable you will do what you can to lighten their sorrows. To find that you do not look upon and speak to them with contempt, but treat them with some degree of kindness and respect, will make them feel not quite so unhappy, perhaps, as they did before.

This is the end of the sermon.—*Jacob Abbott.*

160. Repeat the "text" of Mr. Abbott's sermon.
161. Repeat the "illustration."
162. Give the "application" of the sermon.
The next two questions need not be answered aloud.

163. Do you always treat your school-mates with kindness and politeness?

Are you always regardful of the rights and feelings of the servants?

PERSONAL HABITS.

164. What does good society require as to our persons?
That our persons and clothes be neat and clean.

165. What would be the effect should cleanliness be neglected?

1st. A dirty person cannot have much self-respect.

2d. Cannot have the respect of well-bred people.

3d. Cannot be either comfortable or healthy.

THE SKIN.

166. What care must be taken of the skin to keep it soft and clean?

1st. The whole body should often be thoroughly washed.

2d. The face, neck, hands, and wrists should be well washed at least once every day.

3d. We should use soft water, fine soap, and a crash towel.

4th. When the skin is washed clean it should be thoroughly dried to prevent chapping.

THE NAILS.

167. How should the nails be kept?

1st. They should be neatly cut and trimmed.

2d. They should always be kept clean.

3d. They should not be trimmed by biting them.

168. How can the habit of biting the nails be corrected?

Only by care and determination to correct it.

THE HAIR.

169. How can the hair be kept in order?

1st. It should be combed and brushed at least once every day.

2d. The head should be washed now and then thoroughly.

3d. Each boy and girl should have a brush and comb.

4th. It is not polite to borrow a brush and comb.

5th. No oils or pomatums should be put upon the hair; they catch dust and make the head dirty.

THE TEETH.

170. What are the rules for preserving the teeth?

1st. They should be cleaned with a soft brush every day.

2d. They should be kept free from tartar, which crusts about the teeth and makes them decay.

3d. Tooth-picks made of wood or quill should be used, and not metal.

4th. When teeth begin to decay they should be cared for by the dentist.

5th. Tooth-brushes and tooth-picks are not kept to lend.

THE DRESS.

What a Clean Apron did.

Tidy neatness in girls is an attraction quite equal to a pretty face; and it is a *better* recommendation, because a

safer evidence of good qualities of character.   Incidents
like the following are abundant to prove this :
   A lady wanted a trusty little maid to help her take charge
of a baby. Nobody could recommend one, and she hardly
knew where to look for the right kind of girl. One day
she was passing a by-lane, and saw a little girl with a clean
apron holding a baby in the door-way of a small house.
   " That is the maid for me," said the lady. She stopped
and asked the girl for her mother.
   " Mother has gone out to work," was the reply. " Father
is dead, and now mother has to do everything."
   " Should you like to come and live with me ?" asked the
lady.
   " I should like to help mother somehow."
   The lady, more pleased than ever with the tidy looks of
the girl, called to see her mother ; and the end of it was
she took the maid to live with her, and found—what indeed she expected to find—that the neat appearance of her
person showed the neat and orderly bent of her mind. She
had no careless habits, she was no friend to dirt ; but everything she had to do with was folded up and put away, and
kept carefully. The lady finds great comfort in her, and
helps her mother, whose lot is not now so hard as it was.
She smiles when she says, " Sally's recommendation was
her clean apron."

   171. Relate the story of the clean apron.
   172. What are the objects of dress ?
   1st. To secure comfort and to promote health.
   2d. To preserve modesty.
   3d. To please the taste.
   173. What kind of clothing should be worn ?
   We should wear such clothes as are suited to the season,
to our work, and to our manner of living.

174. Is it ever proper for us to wear dirty clothes?

Only while we may be at dirty work.

175. What should we do when the dirty work is done?

We should wash our body and change the clothes.

176. What care should be taken after the dirty work is done?

Care should be taken that no unpleasant odors shall cling to our persons or clothes.

Appearances Deceitful.

Landlords and waiters, who form their estimate of men from looks and clothing, deserve to fall into blunders which mortify their self-conceit. A capital case of this kind happened recently in Germany.

A stranger who arrived at Ragatz to enjoy its healthful springs was heard at the depot to inquire for a vehicle to take him to some hotel. It was a gentleman advanced in age, plainly clad; in fact, his clothes discovered an unusual simplicity. On his arm he bore a travelling-gown, and his baggage was by no means extensive. He had been referred to the Ragatz Hotel, but, being somewhat absent-minded, he mounted the omnibus of the Spring Hotel, at which place it left him.

The porter scrutinized him closely, assigning him rooms on the third story. Soon a waiter knocked and presented the hotel register, in which the old gentleman signed his name and returned him the book. The waiter read the name, when, eying the guest at first with surprise and then in doubt, he ran forthwith to the proprietor of the hotel. Having scarcely observed the name of his guest he ran up-stairs, and entering the room with a low bow, stammered some kind of an apology, saying that the *salons* of the entire first story were at his disposal.

E   4

"I thank you, my friend," answered the stranger; "I find myself very comfortable here, indeed; and, besides, these rooms are cheaper."

Our host retreated, and the stranger, who retained his rooms on the third story, was a person of no less consequence than General Field-Marshal Moltke.

177. Repeat the story of Field-Marshal Moltke.

178. What should be the style of our dress?

It should always be neat and clean, and should be suited to our age and kind of work.

179. What quality of clothes should we wear?

Such as will make others neither envy nor despise us.

180. Is it always safe to judge people by their clothes?

No; for the best people do not always dress in the richest suits, and the worst people sometimes do.

181. Is it safe to judge of children at school by the cleanliness of their clothes? Why?

Mortified.—Mrs. Porter's Bonnet.

If one is careful to avoid the appearance of rudeness, and to treat all persons, no matter how plainly dressed, with politeness, he will be saved from mortification. The bearing of this observation may be seen in an anecdote of Mrs. Porter, of Niagara Falls. She was the wife of General Porter, a distinguished soldier of the war of 1812, and a member of the cabinet of President John Quincy Adams. Mrs. Porter was a lady of many accomplishments, excelling as a housewife, and in the grace and brilliancy which are so attractive in the drawing-room.

Usually she dressed in plain apparel. One day, she stopped to dine at a hotel in Batavia, New York, having driven there in her carriage. Leaving her bonnet, a very plain one, on the table of the sitting-room, she went in to dinner. On her return, she found a gentleman, one of a gay wedding-party, carrying her bonnet on the end of his cane, and offering it for sale at auction. Waiting a few moments, she remarked that if he could not get a satisfactory bid for the bonnet she would take it. Whereupon he tossed it to her, superciliously, as if she were a person as inferior as her bonnet was plain. Mrs. Porter, without noticing the action, entered her carriage and drove to her home at Black Rock.

The next day, the gentlemen of the wedding-party called on General Porter, to whom they had letters of introduction. Mr. Porter invited them and their ladies to dine with him on the following day. At the appointed time the party were shown into the parlor, and in a few minutes General and Mrs. Porter entered. Immediately Mrs. Porter was recognized as the *woman* whose bonnet they had made so much sport of. She, also recognizing the party, received them with a little more than her usual grace and dignity. Not a word was uttered concerning the unfortunate auction, but Mrs. Porter would have been more or less than human if she had not slightly enjoyed their embarrassing mortification. The auctioneer said that he never felt so wretchedly or behaved so awkwardly as at that dinner-table.

182. Relate the story of Mrs. Porter's bonnet.
183. How do modest people always dress?
Modest people dress so as not to attract attention.
184. How do immodest people dress?
185. How do Indians dress?
Indians dress mostly for show, and have no modesty.
186. When shall we follow the fashions in dress?
1st. When the fashion does not injure our health.
2d. When it does not interfere with our comfort.

3d. When it does not shock our modesty.

4th. When not to follow it would attract unpleasant notice.

Church Costume.

An American lady, recently, in London, went to church in a hat, not knowing the English prejudice concerning that article being worn in the sanctuary. All her friends looked at her gravely, and spoke coldly. She could not imagine what was the matter, and asked her husband if there was anything wrong about her head. He scrutinized her, and told her no; but still she could see that it was the object of attention, and that many looked at her askance. Glad when church was out, and not satisfied that something was not out of place or awry, she stopped in at a friend's who had lived lately in London and told her of her embarrassment.

"Why," said her friend, "it is that hat."

"The hat! What is the matter with the hat?" said the young wife, taking it off her head. "My bonnet did not come from Paris, and the hat is a real beauty."

"So it is," was the reply; "but it is a highly improper head-covering to be worn in church,—an abomination to English women. Your wearing it was a serious misdemeanor,—the veriest miss is not allowed to wear a hat to service. Seeing that your hat was wrong, people supposed something was wrong with you. You can wear a hat almost anywhere else, but if you want to go to church in England and be thought respectable, you must put on a bonnet."

187. Relate the story of the hat in church.

LANGUAGE.

188. What language should well-bred people use?

Well-bred people use only polite language.

189. What is meant by polite language?

It is such a choice of words as shall express our thoughts plainly and simply.

"Street Talk."

Men use it, boys shout it, and, what is far worse, young women and girls speak it. The fact that it comes from the "street" does not prevent its entrance into the parlor. In spite of its vulgarity, it is cherished by those who claim to be genteel. Parents and children should aim to banish it from polite society. This incident may teach the way of eradicating the bad habit:

"Learn to talk like a gentleman, my boy. I am sorry to hear you talk 'street talk.' Do quit it."

"What is 'street talk,' papa?"

"What did you just now say to sister?"

"I told her to be quiet."

"But you said 'Hush up,' and said it very loud and rudely. What did you, ten minutes ago, say to Martha?"

"I told her to go out of my way."

"But you did not say it half so nicely as that. You said 'Get out of this.' And I think you called her some name."

Harry looked ashamed, but he answered,—

"I called her a dirty snick."

"Just so. That is what I mean by street talk. All such coarse, vulgar words, and especially the rough tone and manner, you hear on the street. They belong to those boys who have never been taught any better, and to those men

E*

who, though knowing better, yet do not care anything about the better way. But my boy should never use street talk."

190. What is meant by " street talk"?
191. How do persons learn slang, or street talk?
By keeping company with impolite people.
192. Do people always know when they use slang?
No ; sometimes it is done as a habit, without thinking.

SWEARING.

Rowland Hill and the Sea-Captain.

" Once, when I was returning from Ireland," says Rowland Hill, " I found myself much annoyed by the reprobate conduct of the mate and captain, who were both given to the scandalous habit of swearing. First the captain swore at the mate, then the mate swore at the captain, then they both swore at the wind, when I called to them with a strong voice for fair play.

" 'Stop! stop!' said I. 'If you please, gentlemen, let let us have fair play : it is my turn now.'

" ' At what is it your turn, pray?' said the captain.

" ' At swearing,' I replied.

" Well, they waited and waited until their patience was exhausted, and then wanted me to make haste and take my turn. I told them, however, that I had a right to take my own time, and swear at my own convenience.

" To this the captain replied, with a laugh,—

" ' Perhaps you don't mean to take your turn?'

" ' Pardon me, captain,' I answered, ' but I do, as soon as I can find the good of doing so.'

" My friends, I did not hear another oath on the voyage."

193. Relate the story of Rowland Hill and the sea-captain.

194. What does the moral law say about swearing?

The moral law says, "Thou shalt not take the name of the Lord thy God in vain;" "Swear not at all."

195. Why do people use profane language?

1st. Some people swear because they think it makes them appear manly.

2d. Some swear from habit, without thinking.

3d. Some swear when they become angry.

4th. Some swear from downright badness, because they fear not God nor regard man.

A Polite Reproof.

It would be well for men who offend against good morals and good manners if they met with reprovers as ingenious and polite as are shown in the following incident:

A lady riding in a car on the New York Central Railroad was disturbed in her reading by the conversation of two gentlemen occupying the seat just before her. One of them seemed to be a student of some college on his way home for a vacation. He used much profane language, greatly to the annoyance of the lady. She thought she would rebuke him, and, begging pardon for interrupting them, asked the young student if he had studied the languages.

" Yes, madam, I have mastered the languages quite well."

" Do you read and speak Hebrew?"

" Quite fluently."

" Will you be so kind as to do me a small favor?"

" With great pleasure. I am at your service."

" Will you be so kind as to do your swearing in Hebrew?"

We may well suppose the lady was not annoyed any more.

196. Tell how the lady reproved the swearers.

197. Is there any good excuse for swearing?

198. Have persons a right to offend others by swearing in their presence?

A Rebuke.

Too many military men are profane, but there are *some* military men who not only do not indulge in profanity themselves, but know how to rebuke it in others, as is shown in the following incident:

A friend went into Colonel ——'s office the other morning, and bustling up to the stove, observed, " God, ain't it cold?" and he looked at the colonel.

The colonel also looked at him, but made no motion of recognition. The friend seemed embarrassed, and immediately took his leave. Afterwards he met the colonel in his own office.

" Colonel," he said, " why didn't you say something when I spoke to you the other morning?"

" You didn't address me," answered the colonel. " You said, ' God, ain't it cold?' and when a man asks the Almighty a question, he is supposed not to care for outside interference."

The friend stared at the colonel, but the colonel was in earnest and looked back at him without weakening. It was a capital rebuke of a detestable habit, for the moral law declares, " Thou shalt not take the name of the Lord thy God in vain."

199. What was the colonel's rebuke?

The Prayer.

A story is related by Mr. S., a gentleman in one of our cities, who was hurrying home one night after the labors of the day were over, and as he was passing a corner lit up by a street lamp, he noticed several persons standing together who seemed to be engaged in a very animated conversation.

He knew the parties, one of whom was a particular friend, but not wishing to delay he hurried along. As he passed, however, he heard some language that caused him great mortification, which made a strong impression on his mind.

Several days passed before the two friends again met. As they were now alone, Mr. S. remarked in a very serious manner, "I was very much surprised to hear you praying on the street corner a few evenings ago."

"Oh," said the other, "you must be mistaken; I never prayed on the street corner. I'm not a praying man."

"But," Mr. S. persisted, "I cannot be mistaken. I certainly passed you on the corner, and you seemed to be earnestly engaged in prayer. You repeatedly offered the same petition in reference to some subject in which you seemed to feel a deep interest. You frequently asked God Almighty to damn your soul, and I thought it would be a fearful thing if he would answer your terrible prayer."

The man was overwhelmed with shame and confusion, for if he meant what he said it was an awful prayer, and if he did not mean what he said it was a dreadful impiety. In either case he violated the moral law, which says, "Thou shalt not take the name of the Lord thy God in vain."

200. When a man profanely swears that a thing is true, is he more likely to be believed?

No. Because the man who does not fear to swear profanely might not fear to tell a lie. The one is no greater crime than the other.

Silliness of Swearing.

The habit of swearing is as silly as it is wicked. Boys, thinking it mannish, sometimes use oaths to show off their smartness. Rev. Sydney Smith was once conveyed in a stage-coach by a youth who mixed his conversation with

many swear-words. The clerical wit, having endured the
annoyance for some time, determined to punish the youth,
and put a stop to his bad manners. Having asked permission of the company to tell them a story, he said,—

"Once on a time there was a king (*boots, sugar-tongs, and
tinder-boxes !*) who, at a grand ball (*boots, sugar-tongs, and
tinder-boxes !*), picked up the Countess of Shrewsbury's gar-
ter (*boots, sugar-tongs, and tinder-boxes !*), and said, '*Honi
soit qui mal y pense*' (*boots, sugar-tongs, and tinder-boxes !*)."

"Rather old, that story," said the youth; "but what
. . . have boots, sugar-tongs, and tinder-boxes to do with
it?"

"I will tell you, my young friend," replied Smith, "when
you tell me what your oaths have to do with your conversation. In the mean time, allow me to say that that is my
style of swearing."

201. Relate the Rev. Sydney Smith's style of swearing.
202. Which is the better style of swearing?
203. Why did Mr. Smith tell his story in that way?

Afraid to Swear Alone.

The wicked practice of swearing, which is so common as
to offend the ear in every hotel, and almost in every street,
is often mere bravado. Boys think it sounds manly to be
profane, and men think it gives force and character to their
sayings. Unlike most other vices, it is done openly, and is
intended by the swearer for other people's ears.

"I will give you ten dollars," said a man to a profane
swearer, "if you will go into the village graveyard at
twelve o'clock to-night and swear the same oaths you have
just uttered, when you are *alone with God.*"

"Agreed," said the man; "an easy way to make ten dollars."

"Well, come to-morrow and say you did it, and the money is yours."

Midnight came. The man went into the graveyard. It was a night of great darkness. As he entered the cemetery not a sound was heard: all was still as death. Then came the gentleman's words to his mind. "Alone with God!" rang in his ears. He did not dare to utter an oath, but fled from the place, crying, "God be merciful to me a sinner!"

204. Tell the story of the swearer "alone with God."

205. Is it a sign of courage or manliness to swear?

The following four questions need not be answered aloud:

206. Do you use slang or street talk?

207. Do you use profane language?

208. If you do use such language, can you give yourself any good reason why you do it?

209. If you have the habit of using bad language, would it not be well to correct the habit at once?

AN AGREEABLE VOICE.

210. What does the tone of our voice often show?

Our tones of voice often show the habit of the mind, whether we are good-natured or cross.

211. What kind of tones may be cultivated?

A kind, gentle, winning tone or a harsh, unloving one.

212. How do anger and fretfulness always show themselves in the voice?

By a high pitch, loud words, and harsh tones.

213. How may we often control our temper?

By speaking in a low tone.

214. What kind of tones should we cultivate?

Such as show that we are happy and wish to make others happy.

What to do when Angry.

" I get mad so quickly, and then I'm sure to say something that I'm sorry for ever afterwards."

" When angry, count ten before speaking," answered the boy's father.

The next time the boy fell into a fit of anger with one of his school-fellows he remembered the advice of his father, and counted ten. By this time he was able to keep back the hard words that were ready to leap from his tongue, and so saved himself the grief of shame and repentance.

Try this remedy, quick-tempered boys and girls. It is best, of course, not to get angry ; but if you do happen to lose your self-control, then put a seal on your lips, and remain silent until your hot blood has cooled a little.

215. Tell what to do when angry.

216. Are there any other ways of restraining bad temper ?

217. Name other unpleasant tones that people use when they are impolite.

There are the peevish, the whining, the scolding, the impudent, and the angry tones.

The following questions need not be answered aloud :

218. Have you the habit of using any of these disagreeable and impolite tones ?

219. Does it add to your happiness to use such tones ?

220. Does it add to the pleasure of your friends ?

MANNER OF SPEAKING.

221. What should be our manner of speaking to others ?

We should speak in a clear, distinct voice, looking the person to whom we speak in the face.

222. How should we act when we are spoken to ?

1st. We should give attention by looking the person in the face.

2d. We should give a polite and distinct answer.

223. How may we be impolite in our answers?

1st. By not seeming to hear what is said to us.

2d. By not looking at the person speaking to us.

3d. By giving a careless answer.

4th. By speaking indistinctly and in a low tone.

5th. By replying rudely.

Forgetting Names.

The infirmity of forgetting names is a very painful one; but it often arises from not fixing a name in the mind, and then allowing one's self to become confused in attempting to recall it.

There are well-authenticated instances of persons who suddenly found that they could not remember their own names. An ambassador at St. Petersburg was once in this case when calling at a house where he was not known by the servants, and he had to apply to his companion for the necessary information. The names of common things are sometimes strangely forgotten. The wife of an eminent jurist, who consulted Dr. Trousseau, of Paris, told him that her husband would say to her,—

"Give me my—my—my—dear me! my—you know," and he would point to his head.

"Your hat?"

"Yes, my hat."

Sometimes, again, he would ring the bell before going out, and say to the servant,—

"Give me my um—umbrel—umbrel—oh, dear!"

"Your umbrella?"

"Oh, yes; my umbrella."

And yet at the very time his conversation was as sensible
F

as ever. He wrote or read of or discussed most difficult points of law.

A patient will often use a form of circumlocution to express his meaning; thus, one man who could not remember *scissors*, would say, " It is what we cut with."

224. Relate the story of " Forgetting Names."
225. How may such a habit be overcome?

GRACEFULNESS.

226. How shall we acquire habits of gracefulness?
By learning to stand, to walk, and to sit properly.
227. Is it important to learn these things?
Yes, if we wish to make ourselves agreeable to others.

Awkward Habits.

Great men, sometimes from lack of self-confidence, or from nervousness, fall into habits in society, embarrassing to themselves and ludicrous to others. Neander, the famous church historian of Germany, could not lecture to his students without pens on his desk to pull to pieces while he was speaking. If the pens gave out, the lecture gave out also.

An eminent English preacher had an awkward habit in company even more amusing. " He is very eccentric," was the general excuse of his friends. " If excited in conversation, he would spring up in the midst of his talk, twirl himself rapidly round three times, and sit down again without pausing in what he was saying, as if some external action was necessary to let off the force of his excitement. After dinner at the houses of his intimate friends he would rush up and down the room in the vehe- mence of his spirits, and then cast himself on a sofa and throw up his legs in the air." These were strange antics for one of gentle birth, and accustomed from childhood to the best society.

228. Relate the awkward habits above alluded to.

229. Is it a good excuse for awkwardness to say that a man is ignorant of the rules of good breeding?

230. What are some of the rules for standing gracefully?

1st. We should stand erect on both feet.

2d. With head up, and chin in towards the chest.

3d. With shoulders back.

231. What is an ungraceful manner of standing?

1st. With lounging manner, leaning against the wall or door.

2d. With stooping shoulders.

3d. With hands in the pockets.

4th. With one foot upon the other, or in the seat, or upon the rung of a chair.

WALKING GRACEFULLY.

232. What are some of the rules for walking gracefully?

1st. Head erect, and chin drawn in toward the chest.

2d. Shoulders back; hands out of the pockets.

3d. Feet turned out, with step not too long or too short.

233. How shall we walk in company?

We should keep step together and not jostle each other.

SITTING GRACEFULLY.

234. Give some of the rules for sitting politely.

1st. We should sit erect, without lounging or appearing to be tired, weak, or disrespectful.

2d. The feet should never be placed upon a chair or table, or against the wall.

3d. The feet should not be twisted among the rungs of the chair.

4th. The feet should be placed in front of the seat, but not in such a way as to attract notice.

5th. The head should not be leaned against the wall, as it may soil the paper.

235. How should the chair be used?

It should stand upon its four legs, and not be tilted or leaned against the furniture or wall.

THE AGREEABLE COUNTENANCE.

236. Is a pretty face always a pleasing one?

A pretty face may not be a pleasing one unless it appears kind and gentle.

237. What is the difference in expression between the countenances of a bull-dog and a spaniel?

238. What is the difference in character?

239. May the same difference be seen in human faces?

An Ugly Face—But!

The following story is told of the Duchess de Berri:

She was extremely fond of Dieppe, and passed a great deal of her time there in summer; indeed, it is said that the town owes to her fostering patronage the establishment of the workshops for the production of those exquisite ivory carvings which are well known to every stranger that has visited Dieppe.

One summer evening a fisherman met a plainly-dressed lady walking alone on the beach. He ventured to accost her, saying that he had a petition which he wished to present to the Duchess de Berri, but that he did not know how to proceed in order to do so.

" Did you ever see the duchess?" asked the lady.

" No," was the answer; " but I am told that she is very ugly."

" Give me the petition at all events," said the questioner, " and it shall be placed in the hands of the princess herself."

The fisherman complied with the request, and a few days later he was summoned to the villa of the duchess. What was his dismay, on being introduced to the presence of the princess, to find that she was the person to whom he had given his petition! He commenced to stammer forth some incoherent excuse, but Marie Caroline interrupted him.

" Your petition is granted," she said, smiling; " and henceforth, when people say that the Duchess de Berri has an ugly face, do you add, ' but she has also a kind heart.' "

240. Relate the story of the Duchess de Berri.

241. May we always judge of the character by the face?

2/2. May our habits of mind affect the face?

Yes; a bull-dog temper has generally a bull-dog expression.

243. How do some people train their faces?

1st. Some scowl and frown so much that their faces become ugly by habit.

2d. Some laugh and simper until their faces appear as silly as their minds are vacant.

244. How may children learn to appear agreeable?

By always trying to preserve a kind, gentle countenance, at home and at school.

HABITS OF MIND.

245. What must be the habits of a really good man?

The moral law says he should be, " First *Pure;* then *Peaceable; Gentle* and *Easy to be entreated; Full of mercy and good fruits;* without *Partiality,* and without *Hypocrisy.*"

FIRST PURE.

246. What is meant when we speak of a " good-hearted" person?

247. What is meant when it is said a person has a " pure heart"?

248. What blessing is promised the pure in heart?

The moral law says, " Blessed are the pure in heart, for they shall see God."

249. How may we become impure in heart?

1st. By thinking about impure things.

2d. By keeping company with impure people.

3d. By hearing or using impure, vulgar language.

4th. By listening to and enjoying vulgar jokes.

5th. By reading vicious books and papers.

6th. By seeing impure pictures.

250. How do such things affect the heart?

The moral law says, " Evil communications corrupt good manners."

Mischief of Bad Pictures.

Bad books may poison more deeply, but they cannot poison so *quickly* as bad pictures. The chaplain of Newgate prison, in London, speaking in regard to sensational pictures of crime, expresses the very decided opinion that wood-cuts describing murders and other horrors should be forbidden by law. They propagate crime and encourage murder. He confirms this position by this incident in the recent history of the prison :

A soldier shot his corporal, and several military murders and attempts to murder followed in rapid succession. After the commission of one of these murders, the perpetrator, a private soldier, named Taylor, was brought to Newgate for trial while the first Aldershot murderer was there. Tay-. lor was under arrest for breaking barracks, when one of those newspapers which sensationally illustrate crime was brought into the guard-room, with a vivid picture of the Aldershot crime.

Taylor could not read, but he looked at the picture, and his imagination became fascinated and possessed with the crime. On the very next day, during punishment drill, his corporal offended him, and he shot him dead. " That picture," said he, " put it into my head."

This is the history of a good deal of crime. Sensational pictures of criminal tragedies lay hold of the imagination, are dwelt upon, reverted to and revived in fancy, till the weak mind is fascinated, like a poor bird by the eye of the rattlesnake, and then only the opportunity is wanting to reproduce the crime itself and make the criminal.

251. Relate the story of Taylor and the picture.

252. How do people become criminals ?

By criminal thoughts and communications.

A Boy's Career.

The reading of a single bad book has undoubtedly decided the destiny of many a boy forever. Circumstances indicate that the tragic end of young Philip Spencer, one of the alleged mutineers of the United States b.ig " Somers," was traceable to such a beginning.

If there is reason in the saying that he is to be pitied who grows up without knowing the advantage of poverty, Philip Spencer is to be pitied. He never knew a necessary self-denial. His family was rich and fashionable; his father was a busy public man of great political eminence, and little pains or watchfulness was given to the moral training of the active boy. He did what he liked, and *had* what he liked, and from the time he was old enough to interest himself in books, he *read* what he liked.

Kept at school almost from infancy, he entered college at an age when most boys are just beginning their preparatory studies. There his unformed character rapidly developed the fruits of parental neglect and loose example.

Accustomed to wine at his father's table, and indulged with all kinds of unhealthy mental stimulants, he spent a large part of his time in social or solitary dissipation, and, though plentifully supplied with money from home, his continual waste and want of it led him more than once to obtain it of friends by false pretences.

His favorite volume was "The Pirate's Own Book." Its narratives of wild adventure captivated his young fancy, and its bloody details of roving violence and lawless daring held his mind with a fatal fascination.

His whole life and behavior took the complexion of his reading, and when his short and profitless college course came suddenly to an end, he went to sea.

His father, being then Secretary of War, procured him a midshipman's berth in the navy. But his restless spirit could not bear discipline.

Evidence soon appeared that the young man was fomenting mutiny. A list of names written in Greek letters was found upon him, which, with some further suspicious discoveries, served to convict him and several others of plotting to seize the ship and commence a career of piracy.

The vicious longings begotten in the boy from the exciting stories of the "Pirate's Own Book" had almost been realized. He and his confederates were court-martialled and condemned to die. When told his sentence, Philip at first could not believe it; then he broke down, and cried, "It will kill my mother! It will kill my mother!"

He spent the single hour of life allowed to him in perusing the prayer-book. What would he not have given *then* for the uncorrupted and peaceful mind that habits of pure reading and of pious thought bestow?

We drop a tear over the fate of Philip Spencer, hung, at the age of nineteen, at the yard-arm of a man-of-war.

253. Relate the story of Philip Spencer.

254. What were the special causes that led to the mutiny?

255. How should a pure-minded person act when he hears impure language?

256. How should a pure-minded person act when he is shown improper books or pictures?

The four following questions need not be answered aloud:

257. Do you read books or papers filled with stories of murder and outrage?

258. Do you like to hear dreadful stories of crime?

259. Do you like to see pictures of vice or crime?

260. Do you read books or papers that you would be unwilling your parents should see in your hand?

261. What kind of company should we keep if we wish to be pure in heart?

PEACEABLE.

262. What is meant by being peaceable?

263. How many does it take to make a quarrel?

"Where one will not, two cannot make a quarrel."

264. May a peaceable person be brave?

Yes. A brave man never seeks a quarrel; the bravest are the most peaceable.

265. Is it the sign of bravery to risk unnecessary danger?

"*His Passionate Temper.*"

A lady visiting the Brooklyn prison on Sunday thus wrote of one of the prisoners who is in confinement for the crime of manslaughter. The story shows the folly and the danger of passionate men carrying concealed weapons. She was accompanied by the chief of police.

"'Do you see that short man, the third in the first row?' he asked.

"Yes, I managed to catch a glimpse of a handsome face, and but a glimpse, for I cannot but fear that these men are some of them sensitive to the glance of a stranger.

"'He is a member of one of the best families, as tradition goes, and not very many years ago was doing a good business in one of the finest of our Southern cities. One evening he got into a dispute with his father-in-law, a choleric old gentleman; words ran high, retorts were bandied between them, and in one moment of high passion the young man took out a revolver and shot at the old captain. Well for him that the wound was not a mortal one.'

"After service I had a talk with this man who offered the strange anomaly, in his disgraceful stripes, of a gentleman in prison. Fluent, handsome, graceful, he won the attention at once. He said his business house used to be on —— Street, Baltimore.

"'Then perhaps you knew my brothers, who are both in business on that street?'

"'What, Charley and Ben! Well, I reckon I did,—

saw them every day, was as intimate with them as with any of my friends.'

"'How long do you stay here?' asked my friend.

"'Well, if I'm not pardoned out—and my people are working hard for me—I must remain three years longer. This is my wife.' And we were introduced to a small, lady-like woman with beautiful eyes, though they looked as if they had shed many and many a tear. I sat down by her side. It was my first experience of the kind.

"'Your husband don't look as if he ought to be here,' I said.

"She shook her head. 'He never would have been but for his passionate temper,' she made sad reply. 'He was brought up in luxury, an only son. He was very wild, and only eighteen when we were married. I was but sixteen.'

"When I expressed surprise at this information, she replied,—

"'Yes, I see it all now. It was unwise to marry so early, and I ought to have known that if he could not govern his temper then, as he could not, our married life would not be a happy one. But oh!'—and tears came into her earnest, dark eyes,—'if he is only a changed man, as I hope, I shall never regret, all my life, that he has been in prison, hard as it is. I have a sweet little girl, four years old. Imagine if you can how terrible it must be to bring her to this place to see her papa.'

"I could fancy that it must be heart-breaking; and I thought I could trace back all this misery to the first few words she had said, 'He was a spoiled child.'"

266. Relate the story of "His Passionate Temper."

267. Are passionate people likely to be peaceable?

268. Do peaceable people generally need to carry weapons?

269. What kind of people usually carry weapons?
Generally those who easily take or give offence.
270. How may passionate persons become peaceable?
By trying to subdue their passionate habit.

How He Did It.

There is enough for a volume or a sermon in the following little incident, and we earnestly commend it to all
afflicted with a bad temper:

A merchant in London had a dispute with a Quaker respecting the settlement of an account. The merchant was
determined to bring the question into court, a proceeding to
which the Quaker objected. Desiring to make a last effort,
the Quaker called at his office one morning, and inquired
of the servant if his master was at home. The merchant,
hearing the inquiry and knowing the voice, called aloud
from the top of the stairs,—

"Tell that rascal that I am not at home!"

The Quaker, looking up toward him, calmly said,
"Well, friend, God put thee in a better mind."

The merchant was struck with the meekness of this reply,
and having more deliberately investigated the matter, became convinced that the Quaker was right and he in the
wrong. He requested to see him, and after acknowledging
his error, he said,—

"I have one question to ask you,—how were you able
with such patience, on various occasions, to bear my abuse?"

"Friend," replied the Quaker, "I will tell thee. I was
naturally as hot and violent as thou art. I knew that to
indulge this temper was sinful, and I found that it was im-
prudent. I observed that men in a passion often speak
loud, and I thought that if I could control my voice I
should repress my passion. I have therefore made it a rule

never to suffer my voice to rise above a certain key, and by a careful observation of this rule I have entirely mastered my natural temper."

271. Relate the story of the cure of the bad temper.
272. Which of the two men showed the better spirit?

A Cure for Loss of Temper.

When M. de Persigny (pronounced Perseen'ye) was French Minister of the Interior, he received a visit one day from a friend, who, on sending up his name, was shown into the great man's sanctum. A warm discussion arose between them. Suddenly an usher entered and handed the minister a note. On opening it, he at once changed his tone of voice, and assumed a quiet and urbane manner. Puzzled at the contents of the note, and the marked effect it had on the minister, his friend cast a furtive glance at it, and perceived that it was simply a blank sheet of paper, without even a scratch upon it. When the interview was ended, and he returned to the anteroom, he interrogated the usher as to the meaning of the note. The usher replied,—

" I will tell you, but you must keep it a profound secret. The minister has naturally a quick temper, and when he becomes excited, wishes me to remind him of it. Hearing his voice just now out here in the anteroom, I wrapped up a sheet of paper and took it in, thus firing off a blank shot as a note of warning."

273. Relate the story of the French minister.
274. Why did the minister need some one to help him to cure his hasty temper?
275. Is a peaceable man necessarily a coward?
276. How many kinds of courage are there?

G

There are two kinds, " moral courage" and " brute courage."

277. What is meant by " moral courage"?

It means that kind of courage which makes a person always dare to do right.

278. What is the only thing a really brave man fears?

He fears to do wrong.

A Brave Act.

The quiet heroism of facing danger merely to do good earns fame for the hero all the more as he does not ask it, nor even make himself known. In describing the fire of 1811 in New York, the *Post* of that city says:

" The lofty spires near by of the ' Brick Meeting,' ' St. Paul's,' and ' St. George's Chapel,' enveloped in the rapidly passing embers, soon became the special objects of watchfulness and anxiety. Thousands of uplifted eyes, and we doubt not prayers, were directed toward these holy tabernacles, now threatened with speedy destruction. And there was cause for fear. Near the ball at the top of the ' Brick Church' a blazing spot was seen outside, and apparently not larger than a man's head. Instantly a thrill of fear evidently ran through the bosoms of thousands crowding the park and the wide area of Chatham Street.

" ' What can we do?' was the universal question. ' What in the world can be done?' was in everybody's mouth.

" The kindling spot could not be reached from the inside of the tall steeple, nor by ladders outside, neither could any fire-engine, however powerful, force the water to that lofty height. With the deepest anxiety, fear, and trembling, all faces were turned in that direction.

" At this moment of alarm and dread, a sailor appeared

on the roof of the church, and very soon was seen climbing up the steeple, hand over hand, by the lightning-rod,— yes, by the rusty slender iron.

"Of course the excitement now became most intense; and the perilous undertaking of the daring man was watched every moment, as he slowly, step by step, grasp by grasp, literally crawled upward by means of his slim conductor.

"Many fears were expressed among the immense crowd, watching every inch of his ascent, for there was no resting-place for hands and feet, and he must hold on or fall and perish; and should he succeed in reaching the burning spot, how could he possibly extinguish it, as water, neither by hose nor buckets, could be sent to his assistance?

"'But where there is a will there is a way,' says the old maxim, and it was at this fearful crisis he reached the kindling spot, and firmly grasping the lightning-rod in one hand, with the other he removed the tarpaulin hat from his head, and with it, literally, blow after blow, thick, strong, and unceasing, extinguished or beat out the fire. Shouts of joy and thanks greeted the noble fellow as he slowly and safely descended to the earth again. The 'Old Brick' was thus preserved from the great conflagration of that Sunday morning. Our hero quickly disappeared in the crowd, and it was said immediately sailed abroad, with the favorable wind then blowing."

279. Relate the story of the sailor's saving the church.

280. What is meant by brute courage?

It is that kind which is able to bear bodily pain.

281. What kind of courage has a rooster or a bull-dog?

282. Which is nobler, moral courage or brute courage?

283. Why has a dog no moral courage?

Because he does not know right from wrong.

Humphry Davy's Bravery.

Great men generally have the moral courage which makes them brave in great emergencies. Sir Humphry Davy, the great English chemist, showed this true courage under trying circumstances. When a young man, he was walking through the streets with a pet dog, named Clo', by his side. On turning a corner he met suddenly a mad dog, with a crowd of men and boys in full chase. There was no chance for escape; but if he had been willing to sacrifice his pet, the mad dog would no doubt have seized and killed Clo', leaving him unharmed. But Humphry instantly caught up the pet in his arms, and looked the furious dog steadily in the face. The dog caught him by the leg, tore his clothes, bit out a piece of the flesh, and dashed madly on. The crowd were shocked at the torn leg, covered with foam from the dog's jaws. But Humphry calmly put down his pet, saying,—

"Well, Clo', you are safe, whatever becomes of your master," took his knife from his pocket, cut out from the wound the flesh covered with the virus, and walked quietly home. Fortunately he suffered no harm, but his cool courage made him famous.

284. Relate the story of Sir Humphry Davy.
285. What kind of courage did he exhibit?
286. May not brute or physical courage be desirable?

Being Laughed At.

When I was quite young, I had a cast in my eye, that quite disfigured me, but I so dreaded physical pain that neither the bribes nor entreaties of my parents could prevail with me to have an operation performed. But on my

way to school one day, I overheard two of my school-mates
making fun of me on account of my eye, and all the rest
joined in the laugh. I went home that evening fully willing to have the doctor sent for, to do what he pleased with
my eye; I could stand anything rather than be laughed at.

If your fear of being laughed at always worked out as
much good as in this case, it would be a very wholesome
feeling; but the fact is that for betraying young people into
evil and for withholding them from good, there is nothing
so powerful as this same fear of being laughed at.

287. Relate the story of the boy who was afraid of being
laughed at.

288. What kinds of cowardice did this boy show?

289. Which is the worse, the fear of pain or the fear of
being laughed at?

290. What kind of courage does it require to stand being
laughed at?

291. Are people generally laughed at for doing right?

Not generally, but sometimes they are.

292. Can you give an instance in school where any one
was laughed at for doing right?

A Noble Fisher-Boy.

The 9th of October, 1877, will be long remembered among
the Labrador fishermen. On that day an awful hurricane
raged along the coast.

One of the fishing-vessels, with a large number of men,
women, and children on board, was caught in the storm,
and tried hard to ride out the hurricane. After a few
hours of fearful suspense she dragged her anchors and was
driven ashore.

With great difficulty all on board were safely landed.
Drenched with rain, blinded by the snow-drifts, shivering
    G*

in the cutting blasts, they found themselves on an uninhabited part of the coast, the nearest huts being nearly five miles distant.

The gloomy night closed in as the last of them was dragged ashore from the wreck. Their only hope lay in endeavoring to reach the distant huts; and in the darkness and storm they staggered on through the trackless wilderness. Who can picture the horrors of that night of suffering to this forlorn band!

When the morning sun shone out nineteen of them lay dead along the shore. A group of three women and two children clasped in one another's arms and half buried in mud was found, all stiff and stark in the icy embrace of death.

During the darkness and confusion of landing a family of four young children were separated from their parents, who sought for them in vain, and at length gave them up for lost.

A boy of fourteen, hearing the cries of these poor little ones, and finding they had no guide or protector, resolved to do what he could to save their lives. To reach the huts with them being impossible, he made the shivering children lie down, locked in each other's arms; then he set to work resolutely, collecting moss, of which, fortunately, there was a large quantity about, and piling this around them, layer upon layer, he at length succeeded in excluding partially the piercing cold.

Fortunately, too, he found on the beach the fragment of an old sail, which he spread over all; and collecting more moss, he increased the rude covering until the poor little sufferers ceased to cry with the bitter cold, and declared themselves more comfortable.

Through all the dreary hours of that awful night that heroic boy stood alone by these children, replacing their covering when the wind scattered it, and cheering them with words of hope. He might have tried to escape with the others, but he would not leave his helpless charge.

At length day dawned ; and then he turned his tottering steps towards the settlement to seek for aid. When about half-way he met the parents of the lost children, wild with grief, coming to search for their dead bodies, as they had no expectation of finding them alive.

The young hero quietly told them what he had done to save them, and by his directions they soon found the spot where they lay. On removing the covering of moss, they found the little creatures snug and warm, and in a refreshing sleep.

What words could picture the wild joy of father and mother at that sight ! But alas ! on their way back, near the spot where they had parted from him, they found the noble boy who had saved their children's lives at the expense of his own lying dead. Nature was exhausted after the fatigue and exposure of the night, and, unable to reach the friendly shelter, he sank down and expired.

293. Relate the story of the fisher-boy.

294. What kind of courage did he possess ?

295. Which was more worthy of admiration, the sailor who saved the children or the one who saved the church ? Why ?

The Heroic Young Sailor.

Among many instances of boy heroism on the sea we have found none more beautiful and impressive than the following, which is taken from the account given by a West India chaplain of the Seamen's Friend Society :

" I must tell you of a feat performed by a sailor-boy in the height of the storm. He was literally a boy, and far better adapted to the duties of the school-room than furling a sail in a storm. But his mother was a widow; he must earn his living, and where better than at sea?

"The ship was rolling fearfully. Some of the rigging got foul the main-mast head, and it was necessary that some one should go up and fix it aright. It was a perilous undertaking.

"I was standing near the mate, when I heard him order the boy to do it.

"The lad lifted his cap, and glanced at the swinging mast, at the boiling, wrathful seas, and at the steady, determined countenance of the mate. He hesitated in silence a moment, then rushing across the deck, he pitched down into the forecastle.

"Perhaps he was gone two minutes. When he returned he laid his hands on the ratlines and went up with a will. My eyes followed him till my head was dizzy, when I turned and remonstrated with the mate for sending the boy aloft.

"'Why did you send him? he cannot come down alive.'

"'I did it,' replied the mate, 'to save life. We've sometimes lost a man overboard, but never a boy. See, how he holds like a squirrel; he is more careful. He will come down safe, I hope.'

"Again I looked, till tears dimmed my eyes, and I was compelled to turn away, expecting every moment to catch a glimpse of his last fall.

"In about fifteen or twenty minutes he came down, and straightening himself up with the conscious pride of having performed a manly act, he walked aft with a smile on his countenance.

"In the course of the day I took occasion to speak to him.

"'Why did you hesitate when ordered aloft?'

"'I went, sir,' said the boy, '*to pray.*'

"'Do you pray?'

"'Yes, sir. I thought that I might not come down alive, and I went to commit my soul to God.'

"'Where did you learn to pray?'

"'At home. My mother wanted me to go to Sabbath-school, and my teacher urged me to pray to God to keep me, and I do.'

"'What was that you had in your jacket?'

"'My Testament, which my teacher gave me. I thought if I did perish I would have the word of God close to my heart.'"

Where in the annals of heroism do we find anything more noble than this?

296. Relate the story of the heroic young sailor.

297. What kinds of courage did he possess?

298. Did the mate do right to order him aloft?

299. Did the boy do right to obey orders?

300. Does being peaceable prevent a person from being brave and manly when danger is to be met and overcome?

THE PEACE-MAKER.

301. Besides being peaceable, what else does the moral law require?

It requires us to make peace, and says, "Blessed are the peace-makers."

302. Do peaceable persons urge others to quarrel?

303. May peaceable persons be forced into a quarrel?

Yes, if in defence of themselves or their friends when attacked.

304. What is our duty when we see others quarrel?

We should make all reasonable efforts to make peace.

305. When should we be willing to take part in a quarrel?

Only when it is necessary to prevent injury to those who are unable to defend themselves.

The following questions need not be answered aloud:

306. Are you peaceable or passionate?

307. Can you control your temper when annoyed?

308. Are you a peace-maker at home and at school?

309. What kind of courage is it that would enable you to dare to leave bad company?

310. Have you the moral courage to dare to do right when you are laughed at?

GENTLE.

311. What is meant by being gentle?

312. What is meant by the term Gentle-man?

It means one who knows and practices the rules of politeness.

313. What is the great rule of politeness?

See question No. 2.

314. What is meant by the word Lady?

The word Lady is applied in this country to a woman of refined feelings and polite manners.

315. What should be the characteristics of every lady and of every gentleman?

See question No. 245.

316. How do gentlemen and gentlewomen—ladies, always behave?

They are always mindful of the rights and feelings of others.

EASY TO BE ENTREATED.

317. What is meant by a person "easy to be entreated"?

One who is polite, courteous, easily dealt with.

318. What would you say of those who are not " easy to be entreated"?

Such people are proud, haughty, and cold in their manners.

319. Are children always easy to be entreated?

No. Some are stubborn and self-willed, and refuse to take good advice.

The two following questions need not be answered aloud:

320. Are you easy to be entreated, or proud, stubborn, and self-willed?

321. Are you willing to take the advice of your parents, teachers, and older friends?

MERCIFUL.

322. What is meant by a person "full of mercy"?

It means one who has a kind heart, who is unwilling to give unnecessary pain to anything living.

323. How may we show our merciful feelings?

By sympathy and relief, if possible.

MERCY TO MANKIND.

324. How shall we show our merciful feelings to mankind?

1st. By helping the needy.

2d. By relieving and helping the sick.

3d. By sympathizing with those who are in distress.

325. How should we feel for the poor and the needy?

We should always treat them as we would wish to be treated in like circumstances.

326. Are people always to blame for being needy?

No. Some are unfortunate and should be pitied.

327. How do persons become unfortunate and poor?

By sickness, by loss of property, or by accident.

328. Who may be blamed for being needy?

They who are lazy, idle, and careless.

The Quaker's Charity.

A certain benevolent Quaker in New York was asked by a poor man for money as charity, or for work. The Quaker observed, " Friend, I do not know what I can give thee to do. Let me see ; thou mayst take my wood that is in the yard up-stairs, and I will give thee half a dollar." This the poor man was glad to do, and the job lasted him till about noon, when he came and told him the work was done, and asked him if he had any more to do. " Why, friend, let me consider," said the queer Quaker. " Oh, thou mayst take the wood down again, and I will give thee another half-dollar."

329. Relate the story of the Quaker's charity.

330. How can we best help the needy?

By giving them work and paying them for their labor.

331. Why did the Quaker have the man carry the wood up-stairs and then carry it down again?

He wished him to earn the dollar, and not to beg it.

332. Do persons deserve charity who can work but who will not?

333. If persons are willing to work and cannot find work to do, are they entitled to charity ?

Helping a Convict.

Many a convict after getting out of prison would lead a respectable life if he could only begin well. But people are afraid of him, and won't trust him or give him employment, and so he falls into roguery again to make out a living. The late Henry Raymond, of the New York *Times,* made a convict honest by lending him ten dollars.

One day, while busy in his room, there appeared to him a man, saying,—

"Is this Mr. Raymond?"

Being assured of this, he continued:

"Can I speak to you a few moments, sir?"

The manuscript was shoved aside.

"I have just come from Sing Sing," hesitated the man.

"Not from the prison, I hope," said the editor, by the way of putting the caller at ease with a joke.

"Yes, sir," said the visitor; "I got my discharge a few days ago."

"Well, my man," said Mr. Raymond, "I hope you were innocent."

"No, sir," replied the convict, "I was guilty. You see, sir, I am an engineer and machinist by trade. I want to lead an honest life, and when I got a place, and at work all very well, some kind friend came along and told my boss that I was a prison-bird, and I had to be out of that. Then I got another place and got well to work, and the same thing happened there. Now I am looking for another job, and I am going to begin by telling what I am, and when I get anything to do I sha'n't lose it in the same way."

"How much is it, my man?" said Mr. Raymond.

"Well, sir," replied the man, "I haven't got the price of a dinner about me now, and I don't know where I am to sleep to-night. I think if I had ten dollars I could get on until I found somebody to take me for what I am worth, and give me some honest work to do. I don't want to go down-hill, sir."

The ten dollars closed that conversation on the instant. Perhaps a year afterwards Mr. Raymond was at a fair of

II

the American Institute, and while looking at some machinery on exhibition a decent man in charge of it approached him and said,—

"Is this Mr. Raymond?"

"Yes," he replied ; "but I don't remember you."

"Don't you remember the man from Sing Sing?"

"No," said Mr. Raymond, "I don't remember any man from Sing Sing."

"Why," said the man from Sing Sing, "don't you recollect?" And then he rehearsed the story here set down, and said he had subsisted on Mr. Raymond's loan until he found employment in his own line with a good man, who knew his story, and was well pleased with him, giving him good wages and steady work in a place of honorable trust and responsibility. Taking a bank-note from his pocket the engineer repaid the borrowed money, saying that he had carried it for some months without finding an opportunity to leave his work and come to town for the purpose.

"It's a good ten dollars, Mr. Raymond, for it's just the cost of saving me from ruin."

When he told the story afterwards Mr. Raymond thought it was cheap, and said he had charged all his other loans to the account of the engineer and balanced it.

334. Relate the story of helping a convict.

335. Did Mr. Raymond do right in helping a convict?

336. Suppose no one would have helped the convict by giving him money or work, what would have happened?

337. What should be done for the deaf-mutes, the blind, the insane, the homeless orphan, and the aged poor?

Schools and homes should be mercifully provided for them.

338. Should there be a difference in the treatment of the needy on account of race or color?

339. Should money be given as charity to those who will spend it for strong drink?

340. What rule should guide us in all our dealings with the poor and unfortunate?

MERCY TO CRIMINALS.

341. Why are prisons built and persons confined in them?

Prisons are built for the confinement of those who violate the laws of the State.

342. Why should law-breakers be confined in prison?

1st. To punish them for their crimes.

2d. For the protection of society.

3d. In the hope that they may reform.

343. May bad men be reformed?

Bad men, like bad boys, may change their bad habits.

344. Are bad men likely to reform their habits?

The longer bad habits are indulged in the less hope there is for reformation, but it is never too late to mend.

345. Is it merciful to punish a man by depriving him of liberty?

1st. It may be a mercy to him to keep him out of mischief and to give him a chance to reform.

2d. It is a mercy to good citizens to confine those who would injure their persons and property.

The Convict and his Cucumber-Vine.

There is always some good left in human nature. Keepers of penitentiaries do well to encourage that,—as we see in cases like this, of a kind-hearted convict and the indulgence allowed him :

A pretty prison story comes from Missouri, where, it appears, a prisoner in the penitentiary, too weak to work, and who had the run of the yard, one day asked the

warden if he could be allowed to cultivate a small corner
in the enclosure.

" What do you want to raise?"

" Cucumbers, sir."

" Why, you can't raise them here; the prisoners would
steal them."

" No, sir," said the man, firmly, " they will not steal one
of them."

" Well, go ahead," said the warden; " if any of the cucumbers are stolen, don't come to me with your complaints."

" You will never hear from me on that score, sir."

The cucumbers were planted, watered, trained, and cultivated, and an immense crop was the result. At last, however, as the fruit grew, it disappeared, and the warden became convinced that the owner sold it for liquor, produce,
or some other contraband article. He directed the man to
be watched, and finally he was detected in the act of carrying his cucumbers to the hospital and giving them to the
poor fellows who in their sickness craved them. Not one
had been stolen.

346. Relate the story of the convict and his cucumber-
vine.

347. Are even bad men entirely lost to all feelings of
kindness and mercy?

348. Is it safe always to trust bad men and boys upon
their promises of reform?

It is not safe to put entire trust in those who have lost
their good name.

349. Should a bad boy in school complain if he is not
trusted and believed? Why?

MERCY TO ANIMALS.

350. For what purposes is it right for us to use animals?

They may be used for labor, for our pleasure, for food, and for clothing.

351. Name some of the animals used in various parts of the world for labor.

352. Name some of the animals in different parts of the world that contribute to man's pleasure.

353. Name some that are used for food.

354. Name some that are used to supply clothing for man.

How the Dumb Creatures loved Him.

A French writer says of an old Bordeaux (pronounced Bor'do) sailor of sixty years ago:

" He was so kind to dumb creatures that I have known his boat was coming sometimes through seeing the pigeons start off seaward, and wheel and hover around her till she touched the landing steps, when, almost before he had stepped on shore, they would perch on his shoulders; and then, when his head appeared above the quay, the goat would come capering down, bleating. Old Tinker, the donkey,—such a rascal that it was said he could open every gate in the parish, and the cattle all knew it, and would follow him, and he had to be tethered,—would, as the old man advanced, whisk his tail, prance, throw back his ears and bray; and the very pig, which was often let loose for a run, would come shambling down, and grunt, and arch his back for a rub, not to speak of the tortoise, which would follow him about, and eat out of his and no other hand."

355. Relate the story of the Bordeaux sailor and his pets.

356. Why did the animals show their joy at his coming?

357. What qualities of heart must a man have to make the animals love him?

н*

Kindness to the Pony.

The *Animal World* gives the following interesting item in relation to the influence which habitual kind treatment has over animals:

"Walking down a country lane the other morning, I heard a gentle whistle behind me, and almost simultaneously a shrill neigh burst upon my ear from the neighboring field. Turning round, I was about to retrace my steps towards a man whom I saw standing by the field gate, about a hundred yards away, and whom I presumed had given the call, when a pony dashed past me at a full gallop on the opposite side of the fence towards the gate, and before I had gone many yards, was being quietly led out by the man. Feeling interested, not to say delighted, at this proof of the power of kindness,—for such I had no doubt was the cause of this ready obedience,—I questioned the man, who, seeing that I was interested, told me that, having been accustomed to groom and feed the animal, he was in the habit of calling it from the fields by the peculiar whistle of which I had just now seen the effect; that many others had likewise tried to call him, but always signally failed, the pony taking not the slightest heed of them. He acknowledged that it was through kindness and attention alone that this was gained. In his absence another groom having to catch the pony would attempt the call, but whistle and chirp as he would, it was no use; he was always obliged to enter the field, basket in hand, and so lure it toward the halter."

358. Relate how the man treated the pony.

359. What are some of the rules for the merciful treatment of domestic animals?

1st. They should be well fed and sheltered.

2d. They should not be overworked or strained beyond their strength.

3d. They should only be punished when they need it, and never when their owner is angry.

4th. They should never be kicked or struck without a reason.

5th. They should never be frightened or teased.

360. State some cases where you have seen animals abused.

361. What effect has merciful, humane treatment upon domestic animals?

362. Does it make any difference in the value of an animal whether it has been treated kindly? Why?

363. Have we a right to treat animals cruelly?

We have no right to cause unnecessary suffering to man or beast.

The Mexican and his Mule.

The average Mexican is not cruel to his mule, though he keeps him on a rather low diet. The same is true of the Arab with his camel. Both men are used to rough fare and coarse food, and they treat their dumb servants about as well as they treat themselves.

The Mexican (says a writer in the *Overland Monthly*) drives his beast by words rather than by the whip, and a good understanding seems to exist between the animal and his master. I one day witnessed an incident illustrative of this fact.

A little mule, drawing a big cart loaded with boxes of wine, in turning the corner of a street came into too close quarters with a post placed there to protect the sidewalk, and brought the vehicle to a sudden stand.

The driver instead of lashing the animal and cursing him, as is too often the case in San Francisco, in the most uncon-cerned manner took out a cigarette, lighted it, leaned against

the nearest door-post, and began to smoke, in the intervals of the puffs chaffing his donkey and laughing good-humoredly at his attempts to free himself from his position. I should translate what he said as something like,—
"You are a pretty fellow! A nice mess you are in! Don't ask me to help you; get out of it as you best can; I'm in no hurry," etc., laughing all the time as the donkey pulled and pulled about enough to break the post down.

The poor little animal seemed to understand all that was said to him, and cocked his ears with a most knowing expression, then in a moment lowering them suddenly he seemed to comprehend the difficulty. Forcing his cart backwards, he gave a sudden turn, pulled himself free of the post, and marched triumphantly on with his load, his master shortly following, lighting another cigarette and applauding the performance.

I applauded, too, and, walking over to the driver, extended my hand to him, saying, " Bravo, old fellow! That's better than beating him."

364. Relate how the Mexican managed his mule.
365. How do savages treat their domestic animals?
They are always cruel and unmerciful.

Rebuked by a Lady.

For several years New York has looked well after the welfare of her dumb animals, thanks to Mr. Bergh. Once, at least, a female helper from abroad came to his aid in the cause of mercy where he and his men were not for the moment at hand. The Portsmouth *Journal* says:

"A large and powerful horse, harnessed to an immense cart loaded with ice, upon which were seated three men, was seen struggling along one of the business streets of New York a few days ago, straining every nerve to draw the heavy burden. Quite a crowd of idlers were following to witness the efforts of the noble animal to perform the cruel task imposed upon him by the brutal driver and his unfeeling companions.

" The horse fell to his knees on the flag-stones of a crosswalk over which he could not drag the overloaded cart. The whip of the driver was swung aloft to descend with a stinging cut upon the flank of the distressed horse, when the crowd opened as if by magic to a graceful lady, whose resolute ' *Don't you strike !*' stayed the cruel arm and saved the terrified and trembling beast from the torturing lash.

" Then with flashing eyes and a calm voice she ordered the men to descend and lighten the load. After her commands were obeyed the lady quietly walked away, the lookers-on respectfully applauding the brave act of the fair stranger."

366. Relate the story about the merciful lady.

367. Which was the more humane, the New York carter or the Mexican with his mule ?

ANIMALS FOR FOOD.

368. How should domestic animals intended for food be treated ?

1st. They should not be overdriven.

2d. They should not be left without food for a long time before they are killed.

3d. They should not be tied, as calves, sheep, and chickens often are, as it stops the circulation of the blood and causes them great pain.

4th. When killed, the killing should be done with as little pain to the animal as possible.

Hunting for Sport.

Shooting harmless birds is an exercise that may make some boys good marksmen, but will make more boys hard-hearted.

Almost every boy who goes gunning, if he can find nothing that he wants to bang away at, considers it the next best thing to kill a few woodpeckers. They look so funny, wrong end up on the side of a tree, bobbing and whacking around the loose bark, that the temptation is strong, and the poor, jolly hammerer has no friends, so *bang!* and down he comes, and he is given to the dog to play with and tear to pieces.

That poor little bird, if over a year old, has killed and eaten many hundred thousands of bugs' larvæ, in the form of grubs and worms, and almost every one of a kind which is injurious to vegetation. The cat-bird, one of our finest singers and a bird that is always sociable if ever permitted to be so, eats a cherry occasionally, and of course he must be banished or suffer death. He pays a better price for every cherry he eats than any fruiterer would dare demand in the market in the worms he destroys, and throws in a complete bird opera several times a day in the bargain.

369. Is it right to hunt animals merely for sport?

No; cruelty is never justifiable; the merciful are never cruel.

370. When is it justifiable to hunt wild animals?

1st. When they can be used as food.

2d. When they furnish skins or feathers for clothing.

3d. When they are injurious to man.

371. Name animals hunted for food; for their skins; for their plumage.

372. Name some animals injurious to men that should be killed.

373. Would it be right to torture or worry a snake when it should be killed?

Injurious animals should be killed, but it is cruel to torture them.

374. Is it right to kill little birds for sport?

375. What are such birds good for?

376. Is it necessary to kill birds in order to learn to shoot?

377. Is pigeon-shooting for sport a merciful enjoyment?

378. Should we blame a dog for chasing the chickens?

No, that is the animal's nature; but he may be trained not to do it.

379. Is it merciful to punish the dog for chasing the chickens?

By punishing him we may teach him to let the chickens alone.

380. What kind of a spirit does it show when boys set dogs or other animals to fighting?

381. What must be the mind of a boy who throws stones at dogs, cats, and chickens for sport?

382. What should be said of boys who torture or frighten any kind of harmless animal?

383. Relate the character of a cruel boy. See question No. 60.

384. What kind of spirit does it show when big boys set little boys to fighting?

Robbing a Bird's-Nest.

One boy has suffered by attempting to rob a bird's-nest. He lived at Bangalore, India, and the newspaper of that place tells the story:

"A European lad named Green, on Sunday last, got upon

a large tree on the other side of the railway station for the purpose of taking away the eggs, as he supposed, from a nest which was on the tree. The nest being a little too high up for the lad to look into, he, from a lower branch, put his hand into the nest, and laid hold of a decent-sized snake. Fancying it to be a young bird, he took it out, and on finding what he had laid hold of, and losing his balance, fell to the ground and dislocated his right arm."

We wish every boy who attempts to rob a bird's-nest might find a snake in it.

385. Relate the story of robbing a bird's-nest.
386. Is it merciful to destroy the nests of harmless birds?

Taming a Squirrel.

It is always interesting to make experiments with birds and animals, to see how far their timidity and shyness may be overcome. Shrewdness and perseverance will generally succeed. Here is a good instance of it:

One day, when returning from the meadow, I saw a small striped squirrel on the wall. The men had just been talking about the little creatures, telling how full of curiosity they were, how they would pop their heads out of their hiding-place at the slightest unusual noise, and how a person might approach quite near to them, by gently tapping on a fence or a wall with a stone.

Here was a good opportunity to try the experiment. I picked up two small stones, and then very carefully approached the squirrel, who seemed to be waiting to see what I would do.

When I had taken a few steps toward him, he darted down into the wall with a chip-r-r, as if to say, "No, you don't!"

I took two or three steps more toward the place where

he had been sitting, stood perfectly still for say three minutes, and then began to tap the stones together, very gently and slowly.

In a short time, up came the little head out of the wall. I stopped tapping, and very carefully took a step or two toward the little fellow, as before. I had now got within six feet of him, when down he went again into the wall, and out of sight.

Immediately, and without noise, I went close to the wall, and lay down on the bank, with my face not two feet from the place where the squirrel had been sitting. I laid several kernels of corn upon the rock, temptingly, and waited as much as ten minutes.

After a while, I took one of the stones, and gave three or four gentle taps upon the wall. No reply. In a moment or two I repeated the noise. Presently, I heard a scratching in the wall, and soon up came the little head, not two feet from me. I wanted to scream with delight, but I did not move an eyelid. There we were, the squirrel and myself, looking into each other's faces for at least half a minute. I could see the little fellow's hurried breathing distinctly.

Once he gave a single chip-r-r, and braced his feet firmly on the rock, as if ready to vanish if I should offer any warlike menace. But I kept perfectly still. And after another good, long stare, the squirrel coolly gathered up the corn I had put down, and, with a farewell chip-r-r, he ran into the wall.

Of course I was delighted with my experiment. You may be sure that I tried it the next day, and with equal success. Only it seemed to me that the little animal showed less fear. Within a week, I could plainly see that he was growing tame. I always fed him at the same place, and about the same time of day, taking good care that the dog was not visible, and no one about but myself.

Not to make my story too long, it will suffice to say that
in less than a month Tommy, as I called my squirrel, would
actually take corn from my hand. But it was not corn all
the time, for the food I gave him was varied occasionally.
Before the autumn leaves fell, the little creature would go
all over my person for his food, and even down into the
great pockets of my frock. I never attempted to catch him,
being sufficiently interested in taming him, without a desire
to make him my prisoner.

387. Relate the story of taming a squirrel.

388. Which should we admire the more, the spirit that
would rob the bird's-nest, or that which would tame the
ground squirrel?

389. Was it better to tame the squirrel and enjoy its
pretty ways or to kill it?

390. Was it more merciful to capture the squirrel or to
have it enjoy its life and liberty?

391. What does the moral law say of humanity to animals?

It says, " a righteous man regardeth the life of his beast,
but the tender mercies of the wicked are cruel."

The three following questions need not be answered aloud:

392. Are you merciful to your parents, your teachers,
and your school-mates?

393. Are you merciful to all the domestic animals?

394. Do you enjoy the killing or maiming of any living
thing?

FRUITS OF GOOD LIVING.

395. A good man like a good tree may be known in what
way?

By his fruit.

396. What is one of the most valuable fruits produced in a good man's life?

Temperance in all things.

397. What is meant by being temperate?

It means freedom from excess in speech, food, and drink.

398. What is meant by intemperate speech?

Intemperate speech is language that is calculated to injure, to excite, or to mislead.

399. What kind of speech shall we call the terms " liar," " villain," " thief," etc.?

400. What is meant by a " perfectly splendid copy-book," " an awfully horrid bonnet," " a dreadful nice day"?

401. If we say of the light of a lamp that it is " perfectly gorgeous," what shall we say of a brilliant sunrise?

402. What is meant by " being almost scared to death," being " pleased to death," or being " utterly exhausted"?

403. Is the above language temperate or intemperate? Why?

404. What kinds of people use such forms of speech?

Either those who are ignorant of good language or extremely careless in what they say.

405. What danger is there in forming habits of intemperate speech?

Either that we lose the credit for accuracy, or possibly for truthfulness.

TEMPERANCE IN FOOD.

406. What is an intemperate eater called?

An intemperate eater is called a glutton.

407. What is intemperance in eating called?

It is called gluttony.

408. Why is gluttony wrong?

Because it is injurious to health.

409. What kinds of food should we use?

Only such kinds as will make us strong and healthy.

410. When and how much food should we eat?

We should eat at regular times, and only take what is good for health and comfort.

411. What is the effect of intemperate eating?

It often produces indigestion, dyspepsia, and distress.

412. Are children ever intemperate in eating, especially at school?

TEMPERANCE IN DRINK.

A Good Temperance Story.

We fear the hotel clerks who would do as this one did are not in the majority. The witty thoughtfulness of the act here described entitles the doer to be called more than "gentlemanly."

About a year ago, eight or ten lumbermen went into a hotel in one of our Western cities and engaged a private parlor. They were jolly, well-to-do fellows, and met to settle up a year's business over a social glass, having had a successful speculation together. Summoning the gentlemanly clerk of the house, they ordered him to bring in the choicest liquor to be obtained,—"nothing but the purest and finest article."

The table was spread, glasses brought out, and mirth and jollity prevailed. Presently in came the clerk with a silver pitcher of ice-water, and as he filled each goblet, with quiet dignity and not a smile on his countenance, he remarked, "Gentlemen, I have done the best I could to obey your order, and here is the purest article to be found in the United States." They were equal to the occasion. Not a word was said till each had his glass before him, filled with the sparkling fluid. Almost simultaneously they all raised their glasses, and pledging each other's health, made the additional one of promising not to drink anything stronger for the year to come. Nearly twelve months have passed, and they have been loyal to their vow. May we not hope that the pledge may be renewed for life!

413. Relate the story of the temperate lumbermen.

414. What kinds of drink should we use?

Only those suited to promote health and comfort.

415. Do people generally become intemperate in the use of water?

416. May persons become intemperate in the use of tea and coffee?

Some people do use these drinks intemperately.

417. What effects does intemperance in the use of tea and coffee sometimes produce?

Nervousness, sleeplessness, and indigestion.

418. Name some of the drinks that produce drunkenness.

419. What are some of the reasons why persons are advised to drink strong drink?

Some " for sociability," some " for medicine," some " to keep out the cold," others " to keep out the heat," some " to give them strength."

420. What was the custom of society about drinking strong drink a hundred years ago?

Drinking strong drink was more common then than now; everybody was expected to drink for sociability.

Refusing to Drink Wine with Washington.

Toward the close of the Revolutionary war, says Dr. Cox, an officer in the army had occasion to transact some business with General Washington, and repaired to Philadelphia for that purpose. Before leaving he received an invitation to dine with the general, which was accepted, and upon entering the room he found himself in the company of a large number of ladies and gentlemen. As they were

ı*

mostly strangers to him, and he was of a naturally modest and unassuming disposition, he took a seat near the foot of the table and refrained from taking an active part in the conversation. Just before the dinner was concluded General Washington called him by name, and requested him to drink a glass of wine with him.

"You will have the goodness to excuse me, general," was the reply, "as I have made it a rule not to take wine."

All eyes were instantly turned upon the young officer, and a murmur of surprise and horror ran around the room. That a person should be so unsocial and so *mean* as to never drink wine was really too bad, but that he should abstain from it on an occasion like that, and even when offered to him by General Washington himself, was perfectly intolerable! Washington saw at once the feelings of his guests, and promptly addressed them.

"Gentlemen," said he, "Mr. —— is right. I do not wish any of my guests to partake of anything against their inclination, and I certainly do not wish them to violate any established *principle* in their social intercourse with me. I honor Mr. —— for his frankness, for his consistency in thus adhering to an established rule which can never do him harm, and for the adoption of which, I have no doubt, he has good and sufficient reasons."

421. Relate the story of Washington's true hospitality.

422. Was General Washington polite?

Yes; according to the custom of the times he was polite in offering to drink wine with his guest, and he was equally polite in accepting his guest's refusal to drink.

423. Is it well for persons unaccustomed to strong drink to take it simply for sociability?

Mr. Greeley and the Brandy.

The following amusing anecdote is related of the late Mr. Greeley, who is known to have been throughout his life a stanch advocate of temperance:

Through all his electioneering campaign he sat at public dinners and suppers where wine and spirits flowed freely, but he never passed the bottle or touched the liquor himself. The waiters who knew his temperance principles were puzzled what to do when they came to the row of glasses fronting his plate. Usually they were directed by a look or gesture of the master of the ceremonies to pass by him in silence, but on one occasion an Irish waiter would not abide such an apparent breach of hospitality.

"Hadn't ye better take something, sir, to get up an appetite like, after your long ride, sir?" the hospitable Hibernian whispered to the startled sage. "A little brandy and wather wad do ye good,—it wad, upon me sowl, sir."

The heartiness of the appeal touched the philosopher. He recognized the ring of true hospitality in its tones, and his heart relented at the idea of depressing such sterling virtue by a continued refusal.

"Brandy and water?" said he. "Well, Pat, I'll take half that to oblige you. Give me the water and let some one else have the brandy."

424. Relate the story of Mr. Greeley and the Irishman.

425. Who was the best judge whether the brandy and water would do him good, Mr. Greeley or the Irish waiter?

Strong Drink as Medicine.

Judge P. was one of the prominent citizens of Southern Indiana. He was a man of good family, of fine education, of elevated social standing, and of high professional character. His fine reputation was recognized by the people in making him their representative in the legislative halls of the State. His professional labors were very arduous, and threatened to impair his health. Feeling very badly, he called on his old family physician, Dr. B., in whom he had great confidence, and asked him what he should do to restore his accustomed strength. The doctor advised him to take a little stimulant every day in the form of brandy, and thought he would not need anything more. The judge commenced to take the prescription regularly. Insensibly the prescribed dose became larger and more frequent, until in the course of several months it became evident to the judge's friends that he was becoming intemperate. Before he himself was aware of it brandy-drinking became a habit that was undermining his health, distressing his family, alarming his friends, and impairing his standing in his profession and in society. Gradually he sunk lower and lower until it was not unusual to see him reeling drunk upon the streets.

Standing in company with some gentlemen on the street one day, with whom was the doctor already alluded to, the conversation drifted in some way to the subject of medical prescriptions. The judge expressed great distrust of the medical profession, " for," said he, " Dr. B. here prescribed brandy as a tonic for me, and I guess he made a mistake."

The doctor was covered with confusion, but replied,—

" Yes, judge, I prescribed that you should take the brandy as a medicine, and now I will give you the prescription that you take it no longer."

" Oh," said the judge, " I took one prescription from you, and I fear it is too late to take another."

426. Relate the story of Judge P. and Dr. B.
427. Why did Judge P. become a drunkard?

See question No. 45.

428. From the experience of Judge P., is it safe to indulge in strong drink as a medicine? Why?

Alcohol and Exposure.

Dr. Brunton, an English physician, says that when men are exposed to cold for a long time the drinking of spirits is exceedingly dangerous. He gives these illustrations in support of his opinion :

"My friend, Dr. Fayer, told me that when crawling through the wet heather in pursuit of deer on a cold day he offered the keeper who accompanied him a pull from his flask. The old man declined, saying, 'No, thank you; it is too cold.'

"The lumberers in Canada who are engaged in felling timber in the pine forests, living there all winter, sleeping in holes dug in the snow, and lying on spruce branches covered with buffalo-robes, allow no spirits in their camp, and destroy any that may be found there.

"The experience of Arctic travellers on this subject is nearly unanimous, and I owe to my friend, Dr. Milner Fothergill, an anecdote which illustrates it in a very striking way : A party of Americans crossing the Sierra Nevada encamped at a spot above the snow-line, and in an exposed situation. Some of them took a good deal of spirits before going to sleep, and they lay down warm and happy; some took a moderate quantity, and they lay down somewhat, but not very, cold; others took none at all, and they lay down very cold and miserable.

"Next morning, however, those who had taken no spirits got up feeling quite well, those who had taken a little got up feeling cold and wretched, and those who had taken a good deal did not get up at all,—they had perished from cold during the night. Those who took no alcohol kept their heart warm at the expense of their skin, and they remained well ; those who took much warmed their skin at the expense of their heart, and died."

429. Relate the story of the travellers who drank spirits to keep out the cold.

430. Why is it dangerous to drink spirits when exposed to the cold ?

"*You Tempted Me.*"

A religious lady at Edinburgh was sent to visit a woman who was dying in consequence of disease brought on by habits of intemperance. The woman had formerly been in the habit of washing in this lady's family, and when she came to the dying woman she remonstrated with her on the folly and wickedness of her conduct in giving way to so dreadful a sin as intemperance. The dying woman said,—

" You have been the author of my intemperance."

" What did you say ?" exclaimed the lady, with pious horror. " I the author of your intemperance ?"

" Yes, ma'am ; I never drank whiskey until I came to wash in your family. You gave me some, saying it would do me good. I felt invigorated, and you gave me some more. When I was at other houses, not so hospitable as yours, I purchased a little, and by and by I found my way to the dram-shop, thinking a little stimulant was necessary to carry me through my hard work. And so by degrees I became what you now see me."

Conceive what this lady felt.

431. Relate the story of the tempted woman.

432. Do people who drink spirits to " keep up their strength" expect to be drunkards ?

433. What is the effect of spirits on the strength ?

434. Is it safe to prescribe strong drink as a medicine?
The moral law says, "Woe unto him that giveth his
neighbor drink, that puttest thy bottle to him, and makest
him drunken also."

" Will you Take the Responsibility ?"

Even the worst of men would shrink from tempting a
fellow-being to his ruin if the consequences involved themselves also; and few would risk it if met at the moment
by the full knowledge of what they were doing.

A young man in Virginia had been sadly intemperate.
He was a man of great talents, fascination, and power, but
he had a passion for brandy which nothing could control.
Often in his walks a friend remonstrated with him, but in
vain ; as often in turn would he urge his friend to take the
social glass in vain. On one occasion the latter agreed to
yield to him; and as they walked up to the bar together,
the barkeeper said,—

"Gentlemen, what will you have?"

"Wine, sir," was the reply.

The glasses were filled, and the friends stood ready to
pledge each other in renewed and constant friendship,
when the young man paused and said to his intemperate
friend,—

"Now, if I drink this glass and become a drunkard,
will you take the responsibility?"

The drunkard looked at him with severity and said,—

"Set down that glass!"

It was set down, and the two walked away without saying a word.

435. Relate the story of the responsibility.
436. Does one glass of spirits make a drunkard?
437. How is the habit of drunkenness acquired?

438. Were those who are drunkards now always
drunkards?

439. Who will be the drunkards a few years hence?

The Infatuation of Appetite.

"Sir, it's no use talking," said a poor inebriate to a
gentleman who was trying to induce him to reform; "if a
jug of whiskey were inside of the 'infernal pit,' guarded
by a line of flame, and I could only get it by passing
through, I'd go for it. I couldn't help it, sir." This
terrible infatuation of appetite was recently illustrated by
a fire in Dublin, Ireland.

The fire originated in a bonded store, in which were
some five thousand barrels of whiskey and other spirits.
The blazing liquid ran down the streets, scattering destruction in its course, until several blocks of buildings were
destroyed. Though no loss of life actually resulted from
the fire itself, two men and a youth fell victims to their
insatiable thirst for whiskey. Soldiers with fixed bayo-
nets guarded the casks rescued from the store; but the
mob found their way into side streets, where the burning
spirits flowed along the gutters like lava. Some, it is said,
tried to collect the liquor in their hats, and others in their
boots, and, failing to satisfy their passionate craving by
such means, they lay across the channels and lapped the
intoxicating stream until about thirty were dragged off to
the hospital insensible, three of whom, as we have already
mentioned, expired.

It is sad to read of such degradation, and to know that
each one of those infatuated men and boys was made so
by taking the first glass.

440. Describe the fire in Dublin, and the effect of the
whiskey upon the men.

441. Are drunkards generally pure, gentle, easy to be entreated, full of mercy and good fruits?

442. Did ever a person drink spirits who intended to be a drunkard?

The Monkey and the Drunkard.

Mr. Pollard states that in his drinking days he was the companion of a man in Arundel County, Maryland, who had a monkey which he valued at a thousand dollars. "We always took him out on our chestnut-parties. He shook off all our chestnuts for us, and where he could not shake them off, he would go to the very end of the limb and knock them off with his fist.

"One day we stopped at a tavern and drank freely. About half a glass of whiskey was left, and Jack took the glass and drank it all. Soon he was merry, skipped, hopped, and danced, and set us all in a roar of laughter. Jack was drunk. We all agreed, six of us, that we would come to the tavern next day and get Jack drunk again, and have sport all day. I called at my friend's house next morning, and went out for Jack. Instead of being as usual on his box, he was not to be seen. We looked inside, and he was crouched up in a heap. 'Come out here,' said his master. Jack came out on three legs; his fore-paw was placed on the side of his head: Jack had the headache; I knew what was the matter with him. He felt just as I felt many a morning. Jack was sick and couldn't go. So we waited three days. We then went, and while drinking, a glass was provided for Jack. But where was he? Skulking behind the chairs. 'Come here, Jack, and drink,' said his master, holding out the glass to him. Jack retreated, and as the door was opened slipped out, and in a moment was on top of the house. His master went out to call him down, but he would not come.

K

He got a cowhide and shook it at him. Jack sat on the ridge-pole and refused to obey. His master got a gun and pointed it at him. A monkey is much afraid of a gun. Jack slipped over the back side of the house. His master then got two guns, and had one pointed on each side of the house, when the monkey, seeing his bad predicament, at once whipped up the chimney, and got down in one of the flues, holding on by his fore-paws. The master was beaten. The man kept that monkey twelve years, but could never persuade him to taste another drop of whiskey. The beast had more sense than a man."

443. Relate the story of the drunken monkey.

444. Why would not the monkey drink again?

445. Could such a monkey ever become a drunkard?

446. What is the difference between many men and that monkey?

A Sad Story.

The Kansas City *News* tells a sad story of one of those wrecks of noble manhood brought about by the demon of alcoholic appetite. Boys, touch not, taste not, handle not.

" To-day there is a man going about the streets of Kansas City ragged, dirty, and penniless, subsisting on free lunches and the charities of gamblers, who has not slept in a bed for months, and who, during the war, was one of the most dashing cavalry officers in the Union army. He was pro- moted from the rank of first lieutenant to full brigadier and brevet major-general for brilliant exploits on the field of battle, and for a long time had a large and important command.

" He has been in Kansas City for two or three months, under an assumed name, being ashamed to dim the bril- liancy of his record in the service of his country by an exhibition of his degradation under his former honored name. He is generally very reticent, having little to do with any one or talking but little, save when 'engineering' for a drink, at which he is remarkably successful.

"The other night, while lying helplessly drunk in the rear part of a Third Street saloon, some men thought to play a joke on him by stealing his shirt, and proceeded to strip him. Underneath his shirt, and suspended by a string around his neck, was a small canvas bag, which the men opened and found to contain his commission as brevet major-general, two congratulatory letters, one from Grant and one from President Lincoln, a photograph of a little girl, and a curl of hair—a 'chestnut shadow'—that doubtless one day crept over the brow of some loved one.

"When these things were discovered even the half-drunken men who found them felt a respect for the man's former greatness and pity for his fallen condition, and quietly returned the bag and contents to where they found them, and replaced the sleeper's clothes upon him. Yesterday a *News* reporter tried to interview the man and endeavor to learn something of his life in the past few years, but he declined to communicate anything.

"He cried like a child when told how his right name and former position were ascertained, and, with tears trickling down his cheeks, said,—

"'For God's sake, sir, don't publish my degradation, or my name, at least, if you are determined to say something about it. It is enough that I know myself how low I have become. Will you promise me that much? It will do no good, but will do my friends a great deal of harm, as, fortunately, they think I died in South America, where I went at the close of the war.'

"Intemperance and the gambling-table, he said, had wrought his ruin."

447. Relate the story of the nameless drunkard.

448. How could a man who was thanked by Lincoln and Grant have fallen so low?

449. Did that man ever expect to be a drunkard?

450. Did he reap the " good fruits" of a well-spent life? Why?

A Cold-Water Hero.

Brevet Major-General George A. Custer, the comrade of " Phil" Sheridan, and a gallant soldier, like Howard, Foote, Farragut, and Stringham, was a thorough temperance man, and needed no whiskey while out on his exhausting expedition down the Yellowstone and through the perilous Black Hills. A young man, brevetted major-general of the United States army when twenty-four years old for gallant service in the field, a hero, fêted and toasted, and in every way tempted, he maintained his principles. The Secretary of War and several other distinguished government officers visited General Custer at Fort Abraham Lincoln. Says the Newark *Daily Advertiser :*

" When the Secretary and his party were approaching the fort the sutler of the post sent to General Custer's headquarters two boxes and one basket of champagne, with a polite note, suggesting that it might be acceptable to his guests. The general immediately returned it, saying ' he neither drank wine himself nor entertained his guests with it.'

" Another incident may not be inappropriate here. While the general was stationed at Fort Ripley, in 1867, he had a severe attack of illness, and the physician prescribed brandy. ' No,' said the general ; ' I will die first.' "

451. Relate the story of General Custer.

452. Could it have been possible for General Custer to have become a drunkard with such principles? Why?

453. Which of the two heroes is the more worthy of imitation, Custer or the man who was ashamed to let his name be known?

454. If Custer could do without spirits in all his hard campaigns, are they necessary?

455. Do wealth, or office, or social position save men from being drunkards? Why?

What Alcohol will do.

The *Sanitarian* tells "What Alcohol will do," thus: "It may seem strange, but it is nevertheless true, that alcohol regularly applied to a thrifty farmer's stomach will remove the boards from the fence, let cattle into his crops, kill his fruit-trees, mortgage his farm, and sow his fields with wild oats and thistles. It will take the paint off his building, break the glass out of the windows and fill them with rags. It will take the gloss from his clothes and polish from his manners, subdue his reason, arouse his passions, bring sorrow and disgrace upon his family, and topple him into a drunkard's grave. It will do this to the artisan and the capitalist, the matron and the maiden, as well as to the farmer, for in its deadly enmity to the human race alcohol is no respecter of persons."

456. Tell what alcohol will do.

457. How will alcohol applied to a man's stomach affect his fences and other property?

458. Why do drunkards rarely reform?

Because they have not generally the strength of principle to resist the habit of intemperance.

459. What are the " mercy and good fruits" that are produced by the drunkard?

An English Girl's Wise Decision.

Firmness, such as appears in the following example, may cost much heartache, but weakness costs much more. The disappointed affection that turns away a tippling suitor is far less misery than the murdered affection of a drunkard's wife.

A young English woman came to an American city to marry a young man to whom she was affianced in England, and who had come to this country two years previous to engage in business. She was to marry him at the home of a friend of her mother, with whom she was stopping.

During the time she was making up her wedding outfit, he came to see her one evening when he was just drunk enough to be foolish. She was shocked and pained beyond measure. She then learned for the first time that he was in the habit of drinking frequently to excess.

She immediately stopped her preparations, and told him she could not marry him. He protested that she would drive him to distraction ; promised never to drink another drop, etc.

"No," she said ; "I dare not trust my future happiness to a man who has formed such a habit. I came three thousand miles to marry the man I loved, and now, rather than marry a drunkard, I will go three thousand miles back again." And she went.

460. Relate the English girl's wise decision.

461. Is it safe to trust the promises of a man who has contracted the habit of drinking spirits? Why?

462. Which would be the harder to break, the evil habit of drinking or the promises of reform?

463. Was it right for the young woman to refuse to marry him after she had promised to be his wife?

It was right, because she did not promise to marry a drunkard.

464. Might she not have married him and helped him to reform?

No wise girl will marry a drunkard and take the risks of his reformation.

465. Is it possible for drunkards to reform?

It is possible; for the grace of God can save even a drunkard.

466. What is necessary to reform a drunkard?

1st. He must sincerely desire to reform.

2d. He must make the effort to reform.

3d. He must shun his drinking companions.

4th. He must shun every temptation to drink spirits.

5th. His friends must try to help him keep his good resolutions.

467. Do all these things always reform a drunkard?

No. Sometimes the habit is too strong to be overcome, and the unfortunate person dies a drunkard.

What Love can do.

This short story, by an English writer, has a beautiful moral. One wonders at the fidelity of the dear child even more than at the brutality of the father:

"That night I was out late; I returned by the Lee cabin about eleven o'clock. As I approached I saw a strange-looking object cowering under the low eaves. A cold rain was falling. I drew near. It was Millie, wet to the skin. Her father had driven her out some hours before; she had lain down to listen for the heavy snoring of his drunken slumbers, so that she might creep back to bed. Before she heard it nature seemed exhausted, and she fell into a troubled sleep, with raindrops pattering upon her.

"I tried to take her home with me, but no; true as a

martyr to his faith, she struggled from me, and returned to
the now dark and silent cabin. Things went on for weeks
and months, but at length Lee grew less violent, even in
his drunken fits, to his self-denying child ; and one day,
when he awoke from a slumber after a debauch, and found
her preparing breakfast for him and singing a childish song,
he turned to her, and, with a tone almost tender, said,—

" ' Millie, what makes you stay with me?'

" ' Because you are my father, and I love you.'

" ' You love me?' repeated the wretched man. 'You
love me !' He looked at his bloated limbs, his soiled and
ragged clothes. ' Love me !' he still murmured ; ' Millie,
what makes you love me? I am a poor drunkard ; everybody else despises me ; why don't you?'

" ' Dear father,' said the girl, with swimming eyes, ' my
mother taught me to love you, and every night she comes
from heaven and stands by my little bed, and says, " Millie,
don't leave your father ; he will get away from that rum
fiend some of these days, and then how happy you will
be." ' The quiet, persistent love of this child was the
redemption of this man."

468. Relate what love can do in reform.

469. Was it the duty of Millie to adhere to her father?

470. How long may we hope and work for the reformation of a drunkard?

As long as he lives.

What He Lost.

Sinful gratification is well worth losing, for nothing
short of its loss leaves room in the heart for a true and
noble life. This is the moral of a reformed young man's
temperance speech recently made in New York, which the
Independent reports as follows :

" I have been thinking, since I came into the meeting to-night, about the losses I've met with since I signed the total abstinence pledge. I tell you, there isn't a man in the society who has lost more by stopping drink than I have. Wait a bit till I tell you what I mean. There was a nice job of work to be done in the shop to-day, and the boss called for me. ' Give it to Law,' says he. ' He's the best hand in the shop.' Well, I told my wife at supper-time, and says she,—

" ' Why, Laurie, he used to call you the worst. You've lost your bad name, haven't you ?'

" ' That's a fact, wife,' says I. ' And it ain't all I've lost in the last sixteen months, either. I had poverty and wretchedness, and I've lost them. I had an old, ragged coat, and a shocking bad hat, and some water-proof boots that let the wet out at the toe as fast as they took it in at the heel. I've lost them. I had a red face, and a trembling hand, and a pair of shaky legs, that gave me an awkward tumble now and then. I had a habit of cursing and swearing, and I've got rid of that. I had an aching head sometimes, and a heavy heart, and, worse than all the rest, a guilty conscience. Thank God, I've lost them all !' Then I told my wife what she had lost. ' You had an old, ragged gown, Mary,' says I. ' And you had trouble, and sorrow, and a poor, wretched home, and plenty of heart-aches, for you had a miserable drunkard for a husband. Mary, Mary, thank the Lord for all you and I have lost since I signed the Good Samaritan pledge !' "

471. Relate what Laurie lost, and how he lost it.

472. State what Laurie gained.

473. If it is not right to learn to drink spirits, is it right to give them or sell them as a drink to others ?

See question No. 90.

474. What does the moral law say about tempting .our neighbor?

" Lead us not into temptation, but deliver us from evil."

475. Repeat the eleventh commandment.

See question No. 80.

476. Is it possible for you to love your neighbor and at the same time tempt him to his ruin?

An Awakened Conscience.

Of all the terrible curses that have destroyed humanity, intemperance is the most fearful :

A young man entered the bar-room of a village tavern and called for a drink. " No," said the landlord, " you have had *delirium tremens* once, and I cannot sell you any more."

He stepped aside to make room for a couple of young men who had just entered, and the landlord waited upon them very politely. The other had stood by, silent and sullen, and when they had finished he walked up to the landlord, and thus addressed him,—

"Six years ago, at their age, I stood where those young men are now,—I was a man with fair prospects. Now, at the age of twenty-eight, I am a wreck, body and mind. You led me to drink. In this room I formed the habit that has been my ruin. Now sell me a few glasses more, and your work will be done! I shall soon be out of the way ; there is no hope for me. But they can be saved. Do not sell it to them. Sell to me and let me die, and the world will be rid of me ; but for heaven's sake sell no more to them !"

The landlord listened, pale and trembling. Setting down his decanter, he exclaimed,—

"God help me! this is the last drop I will ever sell to any one !"

And he kept his word.

477. Relate the story of the awakened conscience.

478. What is meant by " *delirium tremens,*" or, as it is sometimes called, " *mania a potu* "?

It means " trembling insanity," or " insanity from drink."

The Youth's Execution.

The sheriff, says an old man, took out his watch, and said, " If you have anything to say speak now, for you have only five minutes to live."

The young man burst into tears, and said, " I have to die. I had only one little brother, and he had beautiful blue eyes and flaxen hair, and I loved him ; but one day I got drunk, for the first time in my life, and coming home, I found my little brother gathering strawberries in the garden, and I became angry with him without a cause, and killed him at one blow with a rake. I did not know anything about it until next morning when I awoke from sleep, and found myself tied and guarded, and was told that where my little brother was found his hair was clotted with his blood and brains, and he was dead. Whiskey has done this. It has ruined me. I never was drunk but once. I have only one more word to say, and then I am going to my final judge. I say it to young people, *Never! never! never! touch anything that will intoxicate!*" As he pronounced these words he sprang from the box, and was launched into an awful eternity.

479. Relate the story of the youth's execution.
480. Repeat his last words.
481. Is it safe to get drunk even once? Why?
482. Do you need to drink spirits?
483. When will you begin to need to drink spirits?
484. Do you expect to become a drunkard?

485. Why may you not make a temperate use of spirits and not get drunk?

486. How many times can you drink spirits until you form the habit?

487. Are you any smarter or wiser or better than many other young people were who are now drunkards?

488. What is the safe rule for young folks in regard to drinking anything that will intoxicate?

THE TOBACCO HABIT.

489. In what other habit do many people indulge intemperately?

In the use of tobacco.

490. What is tobacco?

It is a plant, the leaves of which are prepared for chewing, smoking, and snuffing.

491. Is it necessary for the health to use tobacco?

No. Many men and most of the women of our country do not use it. It is rarely used for medicine.

492. Do people like the use of tobacco at first?

No. It almost always produces sickness and vomiting.

493. Why do boys begin to use tobacco?

For much the same reason that they learn to swear and to drink spirits: they think it is manly.

494. If it makes people sick, why do they continue to use it?

They persevere in its use until they become accustomed to it.

495. Is tobacco good for young people?

The best medical doctors declare that young people especially should never use tobacco in any form, as it is injurious to the brain, the nervous system, and to the heart.

496. Why do the older people so frequently chew and smoke tobacco?

1st. It is a stimulant, and after using it some time they feel the need of it, as a drunkard feels the need of strong drink.

2d. Then they continue its use as a habit, which is more easily formed than broken.

497. What are the dangers of using such a stimulant?

1st. That it will be used intemperately.

2d. That its intemperate use will injure the health.

3d. It often leads to or increases the desire for strong drink.

498. What other stimulant do drunkards use besides spirits?

Drunkards almost always use tobacco intemperately.

499. Which did they learn to use first?

First the tobacco, then the ardent spirits.

500. Do women and girls generally use tobacco? Why?

501. If it be good for the boys to use tobacco in any form, why is it not equally good for their sisters?

502. What reasons may be given for not using tobacco?

1st. It is not necessary for health.

2d. It is injurious to many persons.

3d. Its use as a stimulant is likely to result in its abuse.

4th. Its odor is offensive to many persons, and we have no right to make ourselves disagreeable.

5th. It is unnecessary and expensive.

A Chance for Saving.

" A penny saved is a penny earned," is one of Poor Richard's proverbs worth remembering by everybody. Any of our readers, when tempted to form the habit of smoking, will do well to think how much they can save by keeping from the habit. Here is a moderate estimate of the saving:

A young gentleman of my acquaintance concluded to

L

commence smoking cigars on his twentieth birthday, but resolved that he would never exceed eight per week, nor pay more than ten cents each for them. I asked him to reckon how much money would be saved by the time he was sixty if he should place the eighty cents per week in the savings-bank every six months and let it lie there, drawing seven per cent. interest. Being quick at figures, he made the calculation, and found the amount to be *eight thousand three hundred and eleven dollars.* "Put that in your pipe and smoke it," young man.

503. Is it wise to spend money for that which may prove an injury?

The following questions need not be answered aloud:

504. Do you use tobacco in any form?

505. Is it needful to use it?

506. Do you use it with the approval of your parents and teacher?

507. Do you buy it or beg it?

508. Why did you commence to use tobacco?

509. Would it not be better to discontinue its use before it becomes an intemperate habit?

510. Is it well for a young person to continue a habit that will consume so much in smoke?

PARTIALITY AND HYPOCRISY.

511. What have already been discussed as the habits of a really good man?

The moral law says he should be "First Pure; then Peaceable; Gentle, and Easy to be Entreated; Full of Mercy and Good Fruits."

512. What are the remaining qualities that the moral law says should distinguish a good man?

He should be " Without Partiality and Without Hypocrisy."

513. What is meant by persons without partiality and without hypocrisy?

It means that men should be just in their opinions and honest in their dealings.

PARTIALITY.

514. What is meant by partiality?

It means an unjust preference or favoritism.

515. How may partiality be shown?

It may be shown as a false witness, a gossip, a slanderer, and a tattler.

The False Witness.

In the county of Washington, Pennsylvania, a jury of three persons, called arbitrators, was summoned to try a case between two neighbors in reference to some property in dispute. The lawsuit had awakened a considerable interest in the community, and a large number of persons had assembled to hear the trial. The property was valuable, and, as there were many witnesses, the cost of the suit would amount to such a sum as to make it very desirable for either party to win the case. From the anxiety manifested by one of the parties to secure certain witnesses, it was strongly suspected that an effort would be made to gain an award as the result of false swearing. One of these witnesses was just entering upon manhood, and from various circumstances it was supposed that the award would rest to a great extent upon his testimony. His reputation was not the best in the community, so that it was feared his honesty would not offer a serious opposition to a false oath, if he thought he would be well paid for his partiality.

The case was called, and several witnesses took the oath and gave their testimony. Finally the young man was brought upon the witness-stand. All eyes were centred upon him, and expectation was awakened as to what he would say. He was requested to hold up his right hand and take the witness's oath. There was a solemn stillness in the room as he gave in detail all the minute circumstances of the case, as he had been previously instructed to do. The character of his testimony only showed to the opposite party the desperation with which the case was contested, and the baseness of the means employed to secure the desired result.

When the witness was to be cross-questioned or examined by the other side, the lawyer said to the witness, " Young man, do you know the nature of an oath? Do you know that you held up your right hand in the presence of this court and called upon God to witness that you were ' to tell the truth, the whole truth, and nothing but the truth, as you will have to answer to God at the great day'? Young man, do you know the fearful guilt which you incur by taking such an oath, and then deliberately giving such testimony as you have just given?"

There was a fearful silence in the room, which was revealed by the ticking of the clock. Every eye in the room was riveted on the witness. He felt that he was in a position of terrible responsibility; he became restless, grew white and ghastly, and in a moment the strength left his knees, and he fell to the floor as one struck by death.

It was indeed too true, as was afterwards ascertained, that he had been engaged to swear falsely.

516. Relate the story of the false witness.

517. What is a witness expected to tell?

He is expected only to tell what he knows,—that is, what he has himself seen or heard.

518. What is an oath as taken in court?

It is a solemn promise or pledge, by the help of God, to tell " the truth, the whole truth, and nothing but the truth."

519. What is the crime of taking a false oath called?

It is called perjury, and he who takes a false oath is called a perjurer.

520. What is the difference between a perjurer and any other liar?

The perjurer is a liar who solemnly calls on God to witness his lying.

521. Are good men impelled to tell the truth by taking an oath?

No. Good men always tell the truth with or without an oath.

522. What do the interests of truth always require of every witness?

That he tell the truth " without partiality."

The Senator's Oath.

Mr. J. T. was elected a senator from the county of Columbiana to the second General Assembly of the State of Ohio. He appeared and made the necessary oath, and took his seat. In a few days he became melancholy, which soon progressed to insanity. In his insane ravings he disclosed that he was not thirty years of age when he took the oath of office and his seat, and that his conscience upbraided him with the crime of perjury in taking an oath to support the constitution, and at the same moment taking a seat in violation of its provisions. From this insanity he never recovered, and survived its commencement but a few months.

L*

523. Relate the story of the senator's oath.

524. Why did the young man before alluded to fall fainting, and the senator become crazy?

525. What is conscience?

See question No. 30.

526. May a witness be compelled to give testimony in court?

Yes. The court may require him to tell what he knows in any case, or go to prison for his refusal.

527. May a man be compelled to testify against himself?

No man is expected to testify against himself, though he may acknowledge his guilt when charged with crime.

528. Why should the court compel a witness to give testimony concerning others?

Because the interests of society require that every man shall tell what he knows when he is called upon.

THE GOSSIP.

529. What is meant by gossip?

It means either idle, thoughtless talk, or a tattling person.

530. How do gossips often harm their neighbors?

By repeating harmful stories about them and creating scandal.

Need of Watching.

Dr. Johnson, giving advice to an intimate friend, said, " Above all, accustom your children constantly to tell the truth, without varying in any circumstance." A lady present emphatically exclaimed, " Nay, this is too much ; for a little variation in narrative must happen a thousand times a day if one is not perpetually watching." "Well, madame," replied the doctor, " and you ought to be perpetually watching. It is more from carelessness about truth than from intentional lying that there is so much falsehood in the world."

531. Repeat Dr. Johnson's advice.

532. May we repeat a scandal about our neighbor even if it be true?

The moral law says, "Love worketh no ill to our neighbor." If we can do him no good, we should do him no harm.

533. When two persons listen to the same story can they repeat it in the same words?

Few people can remember the exact words as they are spoken.

534. How many persons does it take to make a scandal?

It takes two,—one gossip to tell it and another to listen to it.

535. How may we help to prevent gossips from doing harm?

By not hearing and by not repeating anything that will harm our neighbor.

The Origin of Scandal.

Said Mrs. A.
To Mrs. J.,
In quite a confidential way,
"It seems to me
That Mrs. B.
Takes too much—something—in her tea."
And Mrs. J.
To Mrs. K.,
That night was overheard to say—
She grieved to touch
Upon it much,
But "Mrs. B. took—such and such!"
Then Mrs. K.
Went straight away
And told a friend, the self-same day,

" 'Twas sad to think"—
Here came a wink—
" That Mrs. B. was fond of drink."
The friend's disgust
Was such she must
Inform a lady, " which she nussed,"
" That Mrs. B.
At half-past three
Was that far gone she couldn't see!"
This lady we
Have mentioned, she
Gave needle-work to Mrs. B.,
And at such news
Could scarcely choose
But further needle-work refuse.
Then Mrs. B.,
As you'll agree,
Quite properly—she said, said she,
That she would track
The scandal back
To those who made her look so black.
Through Mrs. K.
And Mrs. J.
She got at last to Mrs. A.,
And asked her why,
With cruel lie,
She painted her so deep a dye?
Said Mrs. A.,
In sore dismay,
" I no such thing could ever say,
I said that you
Had stouter grew
On too much sugar,—which you do!"

536. How did the scandal about Mrs. B. commence?

537. How did it grow?

538. How did it end?

539. If the gossips had practised the Golden Rule would Mrs. B. have suffered any wrong? Why?

The Gossip Rebuked.

Dr. Gill, a learned English divine of the last century, was not renowned for his jokes. But he got one off which is quite humorous. Mr. Spurgeon tells the story.

It is said that a garrulous dame once called upon him to find fault with the excessive length of his white bands. " Well, well," said the doctor, " what do you think is the right length? Make them as long or as short as you like."

The lady expressed her delight; she was sure her dear pastor would grant her request, and therefore she had brought her scissors with her, and would do the trimming at once. Accordingly, snip, snip, and the thing was done, and the bibs returned.

" Now," said the doctor, " my good sister, you must do me a good turn also."

" Yes, that I will, doctor. What can it be?"

" Well, you have something about you which is a deal too long, and I should like to see it shorter."

" Indeed, dear sir, I will not hesitate," said the dame. " What is it? Here are the scissors, use them as you please."

" Come, then," said the pastor, " good sister, put out your tongue."

We have often pictured him sitting in the old chair which is preserved in our vestry, and thus quietly rebuking the gossip.

540. Relate how Dr. Gill rebuked the gossip.

541. What was the matter with the woman's tongue?

542. Why is a gossip's tongue dangerous to society?

543. Which are worse, the gossip's itching ears or slanderous tongue?

A Life Ruined by a Slander.

More than fifty years ago a young man lived in a Western city. As a druggist he was accumulating property, possessing the respect and confidence of the community, as was proved by the fact that, as he was about starting to the East to lay in stock, the cashier of a bank handed him a package of money in bills to be handed to a bank officer in Philadelphia.

Being very obliging, he received the package and promised to deliver it promptly on his arrival. This he did. The cashier of the bank to whom he delivered the bills looked over them hastily, placed them in a drawer, saying it was " correct," and went on with his writing.

Now for the singular sequel. A month later the Western banker came to the young druggist and informed him that a bill was missing.

The young man said he did not know how that could be, for he had delivered the package as he had received it, the banker had looked it over, pronounced it correct, and he thought his responsibility ended there. The facts stood thus : two prominent business men, in responsible positions, on one side, and the unsupported say-so of a young druggist on the other. The odds were too unequal, and the young man was not believed.

The community withdrew their patronage and confidence ; his business was broken up ; he first attempted one thing, then another, but a cloud seemed to hang over him.

Years rolled on. The story was handed down from one to another, and new-comers imbibed the prejudices of the old ; and twenty years later there was an odium attached to his character, so that at the mention of his name there was that falling of the countenance which meant " no confidence."

The young druggist became an old man, but never succeeded in regaining the social position he had lost. He died in disgrace.

544. Relate the story of a life spoiled by a slander.

545. Is it possible that an unaccountable error may occur in business?

546. Who was to blame, the druggist or the cashier or the man who sent the money?

547. If we are without partiality, what shall we do in such a case?

It is best to make no judgment.

The Monarch's Question.

When any one was speaking ill of another in the presence of Peter the Great, he at first listened to him attentively, and then interrupted him. " Is there not," said he, " a fair side also to the character of the person of whom you are speaking? Come, tell me what good qualities you have remarked about him." One would think this monarch had learned that precept, " Speak not evil one of another."

548. Relate the habit of Peter the Great.

549. Should any one be condemned without having a chance to be heard? Why?

550. Should a previous good name have any weight in determining the truth or falsehood of any story?

Too Sure.

Over-certainty, as well as conscious falsehood, has a confusing effect on one's language. The Lewistown (Maine) *Journal* says,—

"There was a sheep-killing case at Auburn the other day. The witness for the plaintiff was a most decided witness. What he knew he was positive about, and he was positive to exactness. Warming up to it, he swore on direct examination that he saw the sheep kill the dog. Subsequently the court, addressing the witness, remarked, 'You testified on your direct examination that you saw the sheep kill the dog. Now, Mr. Witness, are you prepared, on your oath, to testify that this statement is true?'

" 'I am,' replies the witness, with unction.

"*The Court.*—'Will you swear that you saw the sheep kill the dog?'

"*Witness.*—'I am sure of what I saw.'

"*The Court.*—'Then you saw the *sheep* kill the dog?'

"*Witness* (soliloquizing).—'The sheep kill the dog! Did I swear to that? (overwhelmed with confusion.) Oh, I don't mean that! What I saw was the dog kill the sheep.'

"The judge, the learned lawyers, and the intelligent jury, were whelmed in one common burst of laughter."

551. Relate the story of the witness who was too sure.

552. Is it well for a person to be too positive?

It is always well to try to be exact, but even the most exact person may make mistakes.

553. If a person can make mistakes in his own language, is it not possible to make mistakes in quoting other people?

THE TATTLER.

554. What is meant by a tattler?

A tattler is a school gossip; one who repeats scandal to injure another.

555. How should the tattler be esteemed?

The tattler is a mischief-making busybody, to be despised by everybody.

556. What is the difference between a tattler and one who is called on as a witness?

The tattler gladly tells what will injure another without being asked, while a witness only gives evidence when the teacher requires it.

557. What principle should always govern a witness in school as in a court?

Always to tell the truth, without partiality and without hypocrisy.

558. Why should we despise a tattler?

Because he likes to tell evil reports without being required to do so.

A Brave Boy.

What a glorious world we should live in if only all boys, and men too, had the moral courage and nobleness of Bonnie Christie!

Two boys were in a school-room alone together, when some fireworks, contrary to the master's express prohibition, exploded. The one boy denied it; the other, Bonnie Christie, would neither admit nor deny it, and was severely flogged for his obstinacy. When the boys got alone again,—

" Why didn't you deny it?" asked the real delinquent.

" Because there were only we two, and one of us must then have lied," said Bonnie.

" Then why not say I did it?"

" Because you said you didn't, and I would spare the liar."

The boy's heart melted. Bonnie's moral gallantry subdued him.

When school resumed, the young rogue marched up to the master's desk, and said, " Please, sir, I can't bear to be a liar,—I let off the squibs," and burst into tears.

The master's eye glistened on the self-accuser, and the

M

unmerited punishment he had inflicted on his school-mate smote his conscience. Before the whole school, hand in hand with the culprit, as if they were paired in the confession, the master walked down to where Christie sat, and said aloud, with some emotion, "Bonnie, Bonnie, lad, he and I beg your pardon ; we are both to blame!"

The school was hushed and still, as older schools are apt to be when anything true and noble is being done,—so still they might have heard Bonnie's big tear drop proudly on his copy-book, as he sat enjoying the moral triumph which subdued himself as well as the rest; and when for want of something else to say he gently cried, "Master forever!" the glorious shout of the scholars filled the old man's eyes with something behind his spectacles, which made him wipe them before he resumed his chair.

559. Relate the story of Bonnie Christie.

560. Has the teacher a right to call upon a pupil to testify as a witness?

Yes, when the interest of the school requires it.

561. Why did Bonnie refuse to tell?

562. Was it more manly to tell or to refuse?

563. What kind of courage had Bonnie Christie?

See question No. 277.

564. Which was the nobler boy, Bonnie or his school-mate?

565. Should a pupil ever lie to shield a school-mate?

566. Would an honorable boy ever permit another to tell a lie to shield him?

567. Why did the teacher beg Bonnie's pardon?

568. Is it manly and brave to acknowledge a fault? Why?

569. When we have insulted, neglected, or injured any one, what is the best thing to be done?

It is best to confess the fault and ask pardon of the person injured.

570. When a person confesses a fault and asks pardon, what should we do?

Do as we would be done by, forgive and forget.

571. What should we always remember?

We should remember that we too have faults, and be willing to forgive as we would wish to be forgiven.

The following three questions need not be answered aloud:

572. Are you a tattler, a gossip, or a slanderer?

573. Do you repeat ill reports of people which you would not dare to speak in their presence?

574. In all your language, do you speak without partiality and without hypocrisy?

HYPOCRISY.

575. What is the meaning of hypocrisy?

It means false profession, pretence, or deceit.

576. What is a hypocrite?

A hypocrite is one who professes to be what he is not.

577. In what way does the hypocrite most frequently exhibit his hypocrisy?

In professions of honesty which are intended to deceive.

578. By what other terms is the hypocrite known?

The hypocrite may be a liar, a thief, a gambler.

A LIE.

579. What is a lie?

A lie is anything said or done to deceive.

580. What is an untruth?

It is something spoken or written that is not true.

581. When is an untruth not a lie?

When what is said or written is not intended to deceive.

582. What is the difference between an untruth and a lie?

An untruth may be stated in a mistake, a lie is always told to deceive.

583. What is a liar?

A liar is one who has formed the habit of lying. A liar is always a deceiver,—a hypocrite.

The Old Habit.

The following story is told of Timothy Coffin, an eloquent lawyer of New Bedford, which illustrates the old Quaker spirit, and how ready it was to bear testimony against sin :

The lawyer, then quite young, was retained in a case. Not feeling himself prepared to plead, he was desirous of obtaining a postponement. As the court had already protracted its session beyond the usual period, and the jury were getting impatient to be released, he was aware that it would be impossible to procure such a postponement unless he could allege some extraordinary cause.

He had a lively imagination, and quickly formed a plan.

Rising, with his handkerchief to his eyes, he addressed the court in great apparent emotion :

" May it please the court, I have just heard of the dangerous illness of my venerable mother, who is lying at the point of death. Under such circumstances, much as I regret protracting an already lengthened session, I must request that this case be postponed. My feelings are so powerfully agitated that I should be unable to do justice to the case, feeling as I do that my proper place is at the bedside of my mother."

The pathetic appeal was successful. Sympathy for the afflicted counsel pervaded all hearts, and the jurors were not sufficiently hard of heart to wish the business of the court to proceed at such a sacrifice of personal feelings.

The judge, a tender-hearted man, was about to grant the request, when the hush was broken by a shrill voice, which proceeded from a lady in a Quaker bonnet, bending over the railing of the gallery. It was the mother of the eloquent counsel, who, so far from being at the point of death, came without her son's knowledge to hear his argument.

"Timothy! Timothy!" she exclaimed, in a voice which could be heard all over the house,—"Timothy! Timothy! how often have I chastised thee for lying!"

The court-room shook with laughter, and the eloquent counsel sat down completely ashamed.

The case was not postponed.

584. Relate the story of the old habit.

585. How does it appear that he was a habitual liar?

586. What character would such a man have among men of truth and honor?

Lying is Lying.

The business code of morals is often low. Men who are scrupulous in holding to truth and right in social life see no harm in white lies in business, or in slight departures from integrity. They think it impossible to succeed in obtaining wealth in any other way.

In the same spirit, customers will coin lies to drive a good bargain. Mr. Owen gives a striking instance of this in a beautiful woman of good family, in Naples. She saw a fine pattern of moire antique for a dress at a silk-mercer's in Toledo. She coveted it, and determined to have it. But the lowest price was fifty-eight ducats, and

M*

she was reluctant to pay it. She told a deliberate lie to cheapen the price, and this is the way she told it.

" Your friend Pietro," I said to him, " has a piece the very same as this. I told him of yours, and finally he said that rather than I should go away I might have a dress from his for fifty-four ducats."

" Pardon ! the signora must have mistaken. The man has not a piece of moire antique of this quality in his whole stock."

" He had not yesterday, but the piece I saw was from a box he had just opened. On my *honor* it was just as good as this ;" and she continued, " The man was just fool enough to believe me."

Here was a woman of high family, boasting that she had made a good bargain by telling a scandalous falsehood, and pledging her honor to its truth.

If sellers and buyers would remember that lying is always lying, and admits of no apology ; that it is always mean, and base, and cowardly, it might help them to speak the truth under all circumstances.

587. Relate the story of the woman who lied.

588. Had such a woman any proper idea of honor ?

589. What is the difference, in morals, between defrauding the merchant of four ducats by lying and the stealing of the same amount ?

590. Would a lady ever dare to tell a lie?

No, never ! A lady is pure, gentle, easy to be entreated, full of mercy and good fruits, without partiality, and without hypocrisy.

Tell-tale Pumpkin-seeds.

" Be sure your sin will find you out" was never better illustrated than in this incident, related by an old man of himself, in the New York *Sun :*

" More than fifty years ago, my brother George and I were set to stick pumpkin-seeds between the hills of corn. We both wanted to go a-fishing. Our father told us we might go when we had stuck all the seeds we had.

" So we both worked as smart as we could. But the sun was sinking fast in the west, and we decided that our only chance to go a-fishing was to get rid of the pumpkin-seeds in a more expeditious manner. Near by was a big flat stone ; so the stone was raised and the pumpkin-seeds put safely under it, and the stone let back again, to prevent all future exposure. Never, we thought, had two boys more safely buried their secret.

" A-fishing we went, and had good luck ; brought home trout enough for all. Strange to say, when the seeds came up between the hills of corn, about one-third of the field had no vines. One Sunday afternoon we strolled with our good father past said field, and around said flat stone, on every side, was one mass of pumpkin-vines ! We stood confounded. These seeds had all grown out from under the flat stone, and our fault was manifested ! The thing was so ridiculous our kind-hearted father forgave us, on our owning up to the truth, and the whole truth, and asking his forgiveness. It was to us a warning never to try to conceal a fault."

591. Relate the story of the tell-tale pumpkin-seeds.

592. What is the difference between a lie spoken and a lie acted ?

593. Can those who *act* a lie be trusted to *tell* the truth ?

He Could Be Trusted.

Alfred was missing one night about sunset. Mother was getting anxious, for she always wished him to be home early. A neighbor, coming in, said a number of boys had gone to the river to swim, and he thought it likely Alfred was with them.

" No," said his mother, " he promised me he would never go there without my leave, and he always keeps his word."

But seven o'clock came, then eight, and mother was still listening for Alfred's step; but it was half-past eight before his shout and whistle were heard when he ran in at the gate.

" Confess, now," said the neighbor, " that you have been to the river with other boys, and so kept away till late."

How the boy's eyes flashed, and the crimson mounted to his cheeks!

" No, sir; I promised my mother that I would never go there without her leave, and do you think I would tell a falsehood? I helped James to find the cows that had strayed in the woods, and didn't think I should stay so late."

" I think," said the neighbor, turning to the mother, as he took his hat to go home, " there is a comfort in store for you by him. Such a boy as that will make a noble man."

594. Relate the story of the boy who could be trusted.

595. How should every honorable person feel at the charge of lying?

596. Which should we dread the more, the telling of the lie, or the shame of its discovery?

597. Is an unfulfilled promise always a lie?

An unfulfilled promise is always a lie when it is made with an intention to deceive.

THE PROMISE.

Sacredness of a Promise.

An eminent British statesman is said to have traced his own sense of the sacredness of a promise to a curious lesson he got from his father when he was a boy. When home for the holidays, and walking with his father in the garden, his father pointed to a wall which he intended to have pulled down.

"Oh," said the boy, "I should like to see a wall pulled down."

"Well, my boy, you shall," said the father.

The thing, however, escaped his memory, and during the boy's absence a number of improvements were being made, and among them this wall was torn down and a new one built up in its place. When the boy came home and saw it, he said,—

"Oh, father, you promised to let me see that wall torn down."

Instantly the father remembered his promise, and was deeply pained to think that he had seemed careless about his plighted word.

"My boy," he said, "you are right. I did promise, and I ought not to have forgotten. It is too late now to do just what I said I would, but you wanted to see a wall pulled down, and so you shall."

And he actually ordered the masons up, and made them pull down and rebuild the new wall, that as nearly as possible his promise might be made good.

"It cost me twenty pounds," he said to a friend, who was bantering him about it, "but," he said, "if it had cost a hundred I should have thought it a cheap way of impressing on my boy's mind as long as he lives the importance that a man of honor should attach to his plighted word."

598. Relate the story of the sacredness of a promise.

599. What is a promise?

It is an agreement to do or not to do a particular thing.

600. What name may we justly get if we are not careful to keep our promises?

His Promise to Pay.

One day a little son of a well-known bank-officer in Wall Street, New York, lost his purse while coming from Central Park, and a stranger, seeing his discomfort, paid his railroad fare, three cents. The boy, thanking him, said, "If you will tell me your name, sir, I will bring it to you to-morrow."

"Oh, no," said the gentleman, "never mind about it."

The boy persisted, saying his father never allowed him to run in debt.

"I will not give you my name," replied the gentleman, "but I live at No. ——, on —— Street."

The next morning the door-bell rang at that house, and our little hero told the amused servant-maid his errand.

"Which of the gentlemen is it?" said she; "there are several in the family."

The boy twisted on his heel, and, after a moment's thought, said, "Have you a photograph book in this house?"

She brought it, and, after a moment's thought, he said, pointing to one, "That's my man. Please give him three cents, and tell him the boy who borrowed it in the cars yesterday left it to pay his debt."

601. Relate the story of the boy's promise to pay.

602. What habit might be expected from such a boy when he would become a man?

603. What is our duty in making a promise?

It is our duty never to make a promise unless,—

1st. We intend to keep it.

2d. Unless it is likely that we shall not be prevented from keeping it.

604. Should we ever make a promise to do wrong?

As we have no right to do wrong, so we have no right to promise to do wrong.

605. If we promised to do wrong, would it be better to break a bad promise or to do the wrong?

A Promising Shoemaker.

Herr Bismarck teaches good lessons, but he has rough ways of doing it. A Berlin shoemaker, who was proverbial for making promises which he did not keep, was taught to be punctual.

The man, after many express promises, had neglected him on several occasions. When this again occurred, the shoemaker was roused at six o'clock the next morning by a messenger with the simple question,—

" Are Herr von Bismarck's boots ready yet?"

When the maker said " No" he retired ; but in ten minutes another arrived. Loud rang the bell.

" Are Herr von Bismarck's boots ready yet ?"

" No."

And so it went on every ten minutes until the boots were ready in the evening. The shoemaker, no doubt, never disappointed him again.

606. Relate Herr von Bismarck's treatment of the promising shoemaker.

607. What is the lesson taught by Bismarck ?

A Truthful Indian.

Wash-a-kie, the chief of the Snake Indians, seems one of those men who believe in the sacredness of the pledged word. The following incident is related concerning him :

This noble old man, in 1864, when some of his young men, under a rebellious chief, went off to fight the whites, followed them, and remonstrated with them ; and, when they refused to listen to his voice, he sat down, covered his head with his blanket, and mourned for them as for the dead. The old chief soon had his revenge, however, for the rebellious band was caught by General Conner, and nearly all killed. Those who escaped came back, and humbly asked Wash-a-kie to receive them into the tribe again; but he sternly refused, and, for nearly a year, would not see them. At last, softened by the petitions of his people, the old chief pardoned the rebellious warriors, deprived their chief of his authority, received them back, and appointed a new chief over them. All this was done from a conviction of duty, to comply strictly with the terms of his treaty, and show the white Father, as he said, that he " would be his friend at home, as he had promised in the council, and as the white Father had written it on the paper." What a lesson to our government, and to the monarchs of Europe! Where is the king who might not gather wisdom from this savage, and learn to stand by " what he had agreed to in council, and written on the paper"?

608. Relate the story of the truthful Indian.

609. Which was the more worthy of respect, the Indian or the faithless shoemaker? Why?

610. Was the old chief to blame for the conduct of the young men?

The following questions need not be answered aloud:

611. Are you always without hypocrisy?

612. Do you always tell the truth, without fear or favor?

613. What is your promise worth?

614. Do you ever tell a lie as a joke in fun?

615. Do you make promises and forget them?

616. Have you a right to make promises and forget them?

617. Do you keep your engagements?

618. Have you a right to disappoint others in your engagements?

HABITS OF LABOR.

Working for an Education.

One of the most instructive parts of Dr. John Todd's biography is the account of his struggles to obtain a college education. He had nobody to encourage or to help him, but his own intense energy triumphed over the most formidable difficulties. He walked from Charlestown to New Haven, with his entire wardrobe under one arm and his entire library under the other.

Reaching New Haven early in the afternoon, he was at once examined, and found wholly unprepared to enter, but was admitted under the condition of making up his deficiencies by subsequent study. He then started for Guilford to see an uncle, having three cents in his pocket, but hungry as a hawk, having tasted nothing since breakfast. Two cents were paid for toll at a bridge. When night came on, he lay down to sleep under a cedar-tree, and woke in the morning stiff, sore, and almost frozen, but with energy and hope unshaken.

During his college course he was obliged to support himself by teaching, and in various other ways; but in spite of imperfect preparation and of incessant work to pay his way, he was one of the best scholars in his class, and graduated with high honor. His success proves that a resolute will can conquer all obstacles.

619. Relate the story of Dr. Todd's working for an education.

620. Why did young Todd want a college education?

Because he wanted to be fitted for the greatest usefulness.

621. How was he useful when he became a man?

He was successful as a writer of books, a teacher, and a minister of the gospel.

Lyman Beecher as a Peddler.

The elder Beecher had a hard time getting through Yale College. His father was poor and could give him little help, and but for a favorite uncle, Lot, who thought his nephew's genius ought to be trained, he must have abandoned college.

In his senior year all funds had given out, and neither father nor uncle could supply his wants. There was a butlery connected with the college, at which cider, beer, sugar, pipes, and tobacco were sold to the students. Beecher managed to become butler near the close of his senior year, and showed himself a rare business manager.

Instead of waiting for buyers to come to him, he went in search of them. He bought a lot of watermelons and cantaloupes, and wheeled them across the college green in a wheelbarrow, to the great amusement of the students, who took them at once at his prices. Beecher did well by his peddling, paid off all his debts and commencement expenses, bought a new suit of clothes to graduate in, and had one hundred dollars in pocket on leaving college.

He always said he should have been a rich man if he had gone into business.

622. Relate the story of Rev. Dr. Beecher.

623. Why did he think he would have been a rich man if he had gone into trading?

624. What was the effect of his independence and self-reliance?

Improving Opportunities.

Michael Faraday was the most distinguished chemist of his age, and the most popular scientific lecturer. But few men have been less favored of fortune, or have depended more on their own energy for advancement. He became famous only because he made the most of his opportunities.

When a mere boy he was made apprentice to a bookbinder. He was so faithful to his employer that he was permitted to read all the works on chemistry that came to be bound. He remembered all he read, and was eager to prove everything by experiments. As his earnings were small, he could spare only a few pence a week for apparatus. But he made up for lack of money by his own ingenuity. He invented what he could not buy. He made an electrical machine which did good service, having only a glass vial for a cylinder. When he was employed as an assistant by Sir Humphry Davy, he soon knew all that Sir Humphry could teach him, and performed the most difficult experiments as successfully as Sir Humphry.

625. Relate the story of Michael Faraday.

626. Where and how and in what kind of company did he spend his evenings? Why?

627. What was one of the great secrets of the success of Dr. Todd, Dr. Beecher, and Professor Faraday?

They were willing and anxious to work.

The following questions need not be answered aloud:

628. How do you stand in your classes in school?

629. Are you working to secure your education, or are you dependent on the teacher entirely for promotion?

630. Are you regular, punctual, studious, good-tempered, kind, and faithful?

631. What kind of books and papers do you read?

632. What kind of company do you keep?

633. Where do you spend your winter evenings?

PROPERTY.

634. What is meant by property?

Property means anything that may be owned, as lands, goods, or money.

635. How may property be honestly obtained?

Property may be obtained by labor, by purchase, and by gift.

636. What is the first and best means of obtaining property?

By honest labor.

637. What are the different kinds of labor called?

They are called manual labor, dextrous labor, and skilful labor.

638. What is meant by manual labor?

Manual labor is that which is done by the hands. It requires strength of body to perform it.

639. What is meant by dextrous labor?

That which requires skill as well as strength is called dextrous labor.

640. What is meant by skilful labor?

It is labor of the mind as well as of the body. It is thoughtful labor.

641. What kind of a laborer is he who digs a cellar?

642. What kind of a laborer is a blacksmith who shoes a horse? A locomotive engineer?

643. Under which class would the preacher and the teacher come? Why? An architect?

644. Which class of laborers is most common?

645. Which class is fewest in number?

646. Why should everybody learn to labor?

1st. In order to preserve health of body and of mind.

2d. In order to earn an honest living.

Washington at Dorchester.

An anecdote of Washington, told by the Rev. Simeon Locke, who died in 1831, aged eighty-three years, is thus related. Mr. Locke, who was a respected clergyman of Hollis, Maine, was a frequent visitor, about fifty years ago, at a friend's house in Kennebunkport. "When I was a boy," writes Mr. Andrew Walker, the narrator, "I have heard him more than once relate the following anecdote, and I recollect it as distinctly as if told yesterday. He said,—

"'I was a soldier in the army of the Revolution, and was detailed, with others, to build the breastworks on Dorchester Heights. A day or two after the works were begun, General Washington rode into the enclosure. I was a sentinel. Near me was a wheelbarrow and shovel; not far off was an idle soldier.

"'"Why do you not work with the others?" asked Washington, addressing the soldier.

"'"I am a corporal, sir," he replied.

"'The general immediately dismounted, and marched to the barrow, shovelled it full of sand, wheeled it to the breastworks, dumped his load, and returned the empty barrow to its place. Without uttering a word, he mounted his horse and rode away.'"

False pride he despised, and he was always ready to rebuke it.

647. Relate the story of Washington at Dorchester.

648. What lesson did the general wish to teach the corporal?

649. How are the different classes of laborers paid?

n*

They are generally paid in proportion to the time and labor spent in learning their business.

650. Which requires the most labor, time, and expense in preparation, the manual, the dextrous, or the skilful laborer? Why?

651. To which of the three classes do the newspaper editor, the type-setter, and the office-boy belong?

652. What is necessary for success in each of these classes?

Laborers of all kinds, to be successful, must be faithful, honest, painstaking, and true to those who employ them.

653. How is each of these classes respected?

Classes, like individuals, are respected according to their intelligence. The better the education the greater the influence.

The Young Chair-Makers.

A gentleman hearing one remark on the " good luck" of certain boys in obtaining places, replied that it was not " luck" that gave a boy his rise in life, but something else; and then he told the following story:

" My father was a chair manufacturer. He had a very large establishment, and employed many workmen and boys. He used to pay them according to their work,—that is, the number of chairs each made was counted at the end of the week. The chairs were then tried or tested to see if they were well made. If the chair 'passed,' or came up to the regulation, then the man or boy was paid for it.

" In our employ were two boys whose names I well remember,—Rufus Loundes and Henry Mallin. Both worked very well, and hardly ever had a chair fail.

" One day, father wished to select an under-superintendent for the boys' department.

" ' Now,' thought father, ' I desire an honest, conscientious boy.'

" And how do you think he went about finding one ? He assembled all the boys in a large room, and told them that, until further notice, no test would be required ; each boy should make his chairs, and at the end of the week obtain his pay according to the number made.

" ' Now,' thought father, ' I shall discover what boys make their chairs well simply for pay, and what ones do their work for conscience' sake.'

" Father was as good as his word. He found that far more chairs were made than usual, but he paid each boy in full ; yet he carefully marked the chairs, and had those of each boy placed by themselves. At the end of three weeks they were all examined.

" It was discovered that all the chairs of Rufus Loundes were as good as before ; on the average he had not made a larger number, but they were just as strong as ever. Half of Henry Mallin's chairs broke down at the first trial, and those of the other boys were more or less defective. ' Ah,' said father, ' Rufus is my man.' He became under-superintendent, then superintendent, and afterwards a partner."

Doing right when there is no one to watch you but your own conscience is the kind of self-respect that wins the respect and confidence of others and the smile of God.

654. Relate the story of the young chair-maker.

655. What was the real difference between these boys ?

656. Was it luck that gave the boy his promotion ?

657. Is the man who works simply for his wages or the man who works for conscience the one to be trusted ?

Not Ashamed of his Trade.

The snobbishness that despises labor is itself most despicable. Many a noble American has improved the opportunity to rebuke it in courtly society.

On a certain occasion, while Friend Hopper was visiting a wealthy family in Dublin, a note was handed to him, inviting him to dine on the following day. When he had read it aloud, his host remarked,—

" These people are very respectable, but not of the first circle. They belong to our church, but not exactly to our set. The father is a mechanic."

" Well," said Isaac, frankly, " I am a mechanic myself. Perhaps if thou hadst known that fact thou wouldst not have invited me hither."

" Is it possible," exclaimed the host, " that a man of your standing and information can be a mechanic?"

" I followed the business of a tailor for many years," returned the guest. " Look at my hands. The marks of the shears are there still. Some of the mayors of Philadelphia have been mechanics. When I lived there, and while working at my trade, I often walked the streets arm-in-arm with the chief justice. It never occurred to me that either was thus particularly honoring the other, and I don't think it did to him."

The Dublin aristocrat did not give up his hold upon the popular philanthropist, though it is doubtful if he profited further by the lesson of Yankee equality thus presented.

658. Relate the story of the man who was not ashamed of his trade.

659. Is it the trade or occupation that dignifies the man or the character of the man that is worthy of respect? Why?

660. How should laborers of every class be treated?
With reference to their personal worth rather than to
their trade.

Alexis and the Workmen.

The Grand Duke Alexis, son of the Emperor of Russia,
uses his eyes to good purpose. During his walks through
the Bridgeport cartridge factory while on his visit here
some years ago, he pointed to several working-men, and
inquired of Governor Jewell,—

"Are these men what you call in this country the common people?"

The governor replied that they were a fair specimen of
our working-men.

"But do you mean to say that these get into official
positions?"

"Perhaps not any of these men," rejoined Governor
Jewell, "but men of their class do. They are educated
men, most of them; that is, they can all probably read
and write, and most of them take and read the newspapers."

"Do you know of any instances where such men have
actually been elected to office?" again queried the curious
Alexis.

"Oh, certainly," the governor said; "I myself worked
in the shop as a tanner till I was twenty years of age;"
and the announcement seemed to puzzle the duke a good
deal.

Here was the governor of a State, as well dressed and as
well appearing as himself, who had actually worked in a
shop, and this man was welcoming him in behalf of a hundred thousand voters; it was more of an enigma than the
young duke had ciphered on previously; but during his
tour through the country he ascertained upon inquiring

that very many of the public men here have come direct from the workshop.

In Massachusetts, Governor Claflin was a shoemaker, Senator Wilson was a cobbler also, and General Banks was a machinist. In every State just such self-made men can be found. They fill the highest places. President Grant was a tanner, and Vice-President Colfax a printer. President Lincoln split rails for a living. President Johnson was a tailor. There is no end to these examples of promotion.

661. Relate the story of the visit of Alexis.

662. Why was the young duke surprised that mechanics should become useful public men?

Because in his country mechanics are not promoted to public offices.

663. What kind of workmen were Jewell, Claflin, Wilson, Banks, Grant, Colfax, Lincoln, and Johnson?

664. Why do so many persons fail to become dextrous or skilled workmen?

1st. Because they have no manly ambition to excel.

2d. Because they are idle and endeavor to shirk honest work.

3d. Because they need to be watched as they work, and on this account they are never promoted.

665. Why does the skilful laborer generally receive a better compensation than either of the other classes?

Because of the greater labor and expense in securing that kind of business.

Reverses of Fortune.

In our country the reverses of fortune come thickly and suddenly. While Mr. Jewell was postmaster-general, a lady applied to him for a clerkship. Her life and that of Mr. Jewell illustrate the extreme changes that come to many a life.

She is the daughter of a member of the cabinet under a former administration, a gentleman of large means, who lived in great state in Washington, and subsequently was minister to one of the most important courts of Europe, where also he maintained an expensive establishment, as his great wealth justified him in doing.

That was a score of years ago. The war so greatly reduced his fortune that his children are now compelled to labor for their own support.

When Postmaster-General Jewell had respectfully listened to the lady's supplication, he said, in tones of deep sympathy,—

" It makes me sad for you to ask this of me. Twenty years ago, when I was a mechanic, I was in ——, and your father was minister there. I desired to call on him, but doubted the propriety of my doing so under the circumstances. Now you, his daughter, come to me to ask a nine-hundred-dollar appointment. How do I know but what in twenty years my daughter may be compelled to ask a similar favor of one of my successors ?"

666. Relate the story of the reverse of fortune.

667. Is it well to be dependent upon others for support?

No. Every person should be so educated as to be self-supporting in case of necessity.

668. Did the lady spoken of above when a girl have

any reason to expect that she would be compelled to earn her own living? Why?

A Hint for the Girls.

A wood engraver being asked why he did not employ women, replied, " I have employed women very often and I wish I could feel more encouraged. But the truth is that when a young man comes to me and begins his work he feels that it is his life's business. Wife, family, home, happiness, are all to be carved by his hand, and he settles steadily and earnestly to his labor, determined to master it, and with every incitement spurring him on. He cannot marry until he knows his trade. It is exactly the other way with the girl. She may be as poor as the boy, and as wholly dependent upon herself for her living, but she feels that she will probably be married by and by, and then she must give up her wood-engraving. So she goes on listlessly. She has no ambition to excel; she does not feel that her happiness depends on it. She will marry, and then her husband's wages will support her. She may not say so, but she thinks so, and it spoils her work."

669. Relate the story told by the wood engraver.

670. Why are girls less reliable in learning dextrous and skilled labor than boys? Should it be so?

671. When should young people begin to prepare to be useful?

They should begin both at home and at school by learning to study and to work.

672. What habits may be learned at school that are necessary to the successful laborer?

Boys and girls may learn to be neat, orderly, careful, punctual, attentive, studious, and polite.

673. What kind of a laborer do you intend to be, manual, dextrous, or skilful?

674. What does the moral law say on the subject of labor?

" Whatsoever thy hand findeth to do, do it with thy might."

675. What is meant by doing work " with thy might"?

It means that work should be done earnestly, honestly, and faithfully.

676. What must every one do to become an efficient workman?

Work without complaining and without being watched or driven.

677. What wages should a beginner expect?

The wages should depend upon the kind of labor to be performed. The beginner in dextrous and skilful labor cannot expect any wages until he becomes expert.

HABITS OF ECONOMY.

678. What is meant by economy?

It is the careful saving of time and money.

679. Why do so many persons fail in business?

1st. They fail to succeed because they are not good workmen.

2d. Because they do not save what they earn.

Difference between Saving and Spending.

The New Orleans *Picayune* tells the story of a printer who, when his fellow-workmen went out to drink beer, during the working hours, put in the bank the exact

o

amount which he would have spent if he had gone out to drink.

He kept to this resolution for five years. He then examined his bank-account and found that he had on deposit five hundred and twenty-one dollars and eighty-six cents. In the five years he had not lost a day from ill health. Three out of five of his fellow-workmen had in the mean time become drunkards, were worthless as workmen, and were discharged. The water-drinker then bought out the printing-office, went on enlarging his business, and twenty years from the time he began to put by his money was worth one hundred thousand dollars. The story, whether new or old, teaches a lesson which every young mechanic should lay to heart.

680. Relate the story of the economical workman.
681. What are the lessons it teaches?

Beginning Badly.

Hard times compel economy, and they suggest a very common fault among young people,—beginning life with extravagant habits. Most men who acquire large wealth begin prudently, spending little and saving much. The following incident has a moral :

One old gentleman, who had commenced life as a poor boy, had, by mastering the difficult steps to final success, gained considerable wealth as a merchant. When he arrived at old age he retired to private life, to live in ease and comfort on his income, leaving a prosperous business in the hands of his son.

In three years the young man was bankrupt. He had failed in business, and was compelled to take a position as clerk in a stranger's store.

His father was asked why it was that in a business in which he had succeeded so well his son had failed.

He gave this characteristic answer,—

"When I first commenced business my wife and I lived on porridge. As my business increased we had better food, and when I could afford it we had chicken. But, you see, Johnny commenced with the chicken first."

682. Relate the story of beginning badly.

683. How may we waste money?

1st. By buying things we do not need.

2d. By buying carelessly and going in debt.

3d. By living extravagantly.

684. Which was the wiser man, the father who built up the business by economy, or the son who wasted it by extravagance? Why?

685. Was it pride, carelessness, or waste that ruined the young man?

Helping his Wife.

Cases like the following ought to be more frequent among young men beginning life for themselves:

A young man who is highly prized by his employer for his faithful efficiency at his desk, and admired especially by his friends for his thoughtful kindness to his wife, was seen about five o'clock, the other morning, washing the windows of his rented home. A little merriment at his expense elicited the frank response, "Never mind. I can't afford to pay a washerwoman to do it, and perhaps if I demonstrate my ability to take care of a house, the world will let me own one some time." And so he will some time own a house, and be able to hire it cleaned, too.

686. Relate the story of the young man helping his wife.

687. Was it a manly employment to help his wife in that way ?

688. Why do so many men fail in business?

1st. Because they are too lazy to work.

2d. Because they are too proud to live within their means.

3d. Because they are wasteful.

How Money Grows.

Wealth comes from careful savings more than from large earnings. A little laid by every year and put at interest soon counts up. A single deposit, even, grows to handsome proportions.

The Taunton *Gazette* says, " Mr. Le Baron Church has shown us a savings-bank book which teaches a lesson to those who despise the day of small things. A deposit of twenty dollars placed for him by his grandfather in a savings-bank at Newport, Rhode Island, in 1827, and afterwards increased to thirty dollars by the addition of ten dollars in 1832, now amounts to the snug little sum of three hundred and eighty-nine dollars and sixty-three cents. In another year it will be over four hundred dollars."

689. How is it that money is said to grow ?

690. What does the lesson from the savings-bank teach ?

691. What is a miser?

One who saves money for the sake of the money alone, and not on account of the good it may do.

692. Is it necessary to be miserly in order to practise economy ?

1st. No. The economical person buys what he needs ; the miser does not.

2d. The economical man saves what he needs; the miser saves everything.

693. Which is the more to be admired and imitated, the spendthrift or the miser?

Neither is to be admired or imitated.

HABITS OF BUSINESS.

694. What is a bargain or contract?

It is an agreement between two or more persons to do or not to do a certain thing for a price.

695. Is a bargain binding on the persons who make it?

A bargain, like a promise, cannot be broken by an honorable man or woman.

696. May a bargain be changed by agreement?

Yes, if both parties are willing.

697. Can one person compel another to make a bargain?

No, for then it would not be an agreement.

698. Is a contract binding when one of the parties is compelled to make it?

No; both parties must agree to the contract when it is made.

His Word his Bond.

Among the characteristics of a good man described in the fifteenth Psalm is this: " He that sweareth to his own hurt, and changeth not." The late Samuel Brown, Esq., a merchant of Boston, who once owned " Brown's Wharf " and a large amount of real estate, now the property of the Boston Gas-Light Company, seems to have been a man who answered the psalmist's idea. A correspondent of the *Traveller* tells this incident:

" When the elder Quincy was mayor, with his wonderful
sagacity he saw the necessity of moving the almshouse and
the house of correction (then on Leverett Street) to South
Boston. Mr. Brown owned a very large vacant estate
where the buildings now stand, and Mr. Quincy called
upon him and stated his purpose to induce the city government to remove the institutions to South Boston, and asked
the price of the estate referred to. The reply was thirty
thousand dollars. Mr. Quincy said that would do, and
asked thirty days' refusal and a bond on it, in order to endeavor to persuade the city council to agree to the measure.
Mr. Brown replied that he should give no bond, as he said
his word was his bond always. The mayor took his word,
and in twenty-eight days had obtained the proper authority,
and again waited on Mr. Brown, saying that he had come
to complete the sale of that land.

" ' What land ?' said Mr. Brown.

" ' Why, the South Boston land we spoke of,' said the
mayor.

" ' At what price ?' asked the former.

" ' Thirty thousand dollars,' replied the latter ; ' the price
agreed upon."

" ' Did I say that amount, sir ?'

" ' You did.'

" ' Have you any writing to that effect ?'

" ' No, sir, none.'

" ' Well,' said Mr. Brown, ' since you were here I have
been offered sixty thousand dollars cash for it, and can you
expect me to sell it for thirty thousand dollars to the city ?'

" ' I do,' replied Mr. Quincy, ' because you agreed to.'

" ' Have you any proof of that ?'

" ' Yes, I am the witness.'

" ' But you, being an interested party, can't be a witness.
Have you any other witness or proof, and do you ask me

to refuse sixty thousand dollars for the land and sell it to the city for thirty thousand dollars ?'

" ' I do.'

" ' You have no bond for it, have you, Mr. Quincy ?'

" ' None, sir, whatever,' replied the mayor, stretching himself up with great dignity,—' none whatever but your word, and that you said was your bond.'

" ' And,' replied Mr. Brown, stretching himself up with equal dignity, ' so it is. My word is my bond, and for thirty thousand dollars the land is yours.'

" And it was. The buildings were erected upon that estate, and there they stand, a monument to Mr. Samuel Brown's mercantile integrity.

" To-day that land is worth millions of dollars to this city. Can any person but feel proud of this instance of sterling integrity ? In those times thirty thousand dollars was a fortune, but the world could not bid high enough to bribe Samuel Brown to a mean action."

699. Relate the story of the man whose word was as good as his bond.

700. What is a bond ?

It is an agreement in writing.

701. Does an honest man require any proof to make him stand to his bargain ?

702. If Mayor Quincy had delayed closing the bargain more than thirty days, would Mr. Brown have been bound to sell the land for thirty thousand dollars ? Why ?

703. If a farmer agrees to deliver his corn to a merchant at thirty cents a bushel, and afterwards another merchant offers forty cents, what should the farmer do ?

704. If a merchant promise to pay a farmer thirty cents a bushel for his corn, and finds that he can buy of other farmers for twenty-five cents, what should he do ?

705. If a boy has agreed to work for a man for one hundred dollars a year, and another man offers one hundred and fifty dollars a year, what should he do in honor and good faith?

706. What care should every one take before he makes a bargain?

1st. He should carefully consider whether he can execute his contracts.

2d. He should make the terms of the contract so clear that there need be no dispute about their meaning.

A High Sense of Honor.

The Duke of Wellington had a high sense of honor in all money dealings, and would suffer none of his agents to do a mean thing in his name. His steward once bought some land adjoining his country estate, and was boasting of having made a fine bargain, from the straitened circumstances of the seller

"What did you pay for it?" asked the duke.

"Eight hundred pounds," was the answer.

"And how much was it worth?"

"Eleven hundred pounds," said the steward, rubbing his hands in glee at thought of the good bargain.

"Then take three hundred pounds and carry them to the seller with my compliments, and don't ever venture to talk to me of cheap land again."

The steward was confounded, and could scarcely credit his own ears. The idea that any one could refuse to profit by a sharp bargain, and throw money away in paying more than was agreed on, was hard for him to comprehend.

707. Relate the story of the Duke of Wellington's high sense of honor.

708. Did the steward do right to take advantage of a

man's necessities and get the property for what he knew was less than its worth?

709. Was it right for the duke to pay the three hundred pounds contrary to the terms of the contract?

Is Your Note Good?

A Boston lawyer was called on a short time ago by a boy, who inquired if he had any waste paper to sell. The lawyer had a crisp, keen way of asking questions, and is, moreover, a methodical man. So pulling out a large drawer, he exhibited his stock of waste paper.

" Will you give me twenty-five cents for that?"

The boy looked at the paper doubtingly a moment, and offered fifteen cents.

" Done!" said the lawyer, and the paper was quickly transferred to the bag of the boy, whose eyes sparkled as he lifted the weighty mass.

Not till it was safely stowed away did he announce that he had no money.

" No money! How do you expect to buy paper without money?"

Not prepared to state exactly his plan of operations, the boy made no reply.

" Do you consider your note good?" asked the lawyer.

" Yes, sir."

" Very well; if you say your note's good, I'd just as soon have it as the money; but if it isn't good I don't want it."

The boy affirmed that he considered it good; whereupon the lawyer wrote a note for fifteen cents, which the boy signed legibly, and, lifting the bag of papers, trudged off.

Soon after dinner the little fellow returned, and, producing the money, announced that he had come to pay his note.

"Well," said the lawyer, "this is the first time I ever knew a note to be taken up the day it was given. A boy that will do that is entitled to note and money, too." And, giving him both, sent him on his way with a smiling face and a happy heart.

710. Relate the story of the boy who bought the paper.

711. How much better was the honest boy's note than his promise?

712. Why is it well to put agreements in writing?

Even honest people may forget the terms of a contract, and thus misunderstand each other.

713. Is it right for persons to make a profit in their bargains?

Every trader has a right to a profit in his bargains which are honestly and fairly made, but no one has a right to take an advantage to the injury of his neighbor.

714. What are some of the rules that should govern persons in trade?

The moral law says, 1st. "Thou shalt not defraud thy neighbor, neither rob him.

2d. Ye shall not steal, neither deal falsely.

3d. Neither lie to one another."

Doing Business Honestly.

One marked trait in the business morals of the late A. T. Stewart, the great dry-goods merchant, was his honesty to his customers. It may have been due to policy, or it may have resulted from an ingrain morality,—we prefer to believe the latter,—but it was the corner-stone of his success. An incident told in the New York *Independent* illustrates how early and thoroughly he laid that corner-stone:

"A few years ago, Mr. Stewart, while taking me through his down-town store, and pointing out the different departments of that immense establishment, was induced by a little incident to remark that he remembered distinctly the first piece of goods he sold after opening his store on Broadway, nearly fifty years before.

" ' I really knew nothing about dry goods then,' said Mr. Stewart, ' but I had bought some cheap calicoes, and had hung a piece out at the door to attract customers, as was the way in those days. My only assistant was a young man who had been a salesman in Division Street.

" ' The first customer who came in was a woman, who asked the price of the calico, and then asked if it would wash.

" ' " Certainly it will," said the young man ; and with that assurance the customer made a purchase.

" ' When she had left the store I said to the salesman, " Why did you say that calico would wash, when you know very well that it won't ?"

" ' " Why," said the fellow, " we always do; for if we didn't we couldn't sell any goods."

" ' " Now, mind what I say," I said to my salesman, " if you ever again make a misrepresentation to a customer, I will discharge you immediately. If I cannot do business honestly, I will give up and do something else." ' "

715. Relate the story of A. T. Stewart.

716. Which had the true principle of honesty, Mr. Stewart or his clerk ?

717. Is it necessary to success in business to be a hypocrite and dishonest ? Why ?

718. Why was it bad policy to say the calico would wash when it would not ?

" Honesty is the best policy," for the woman being deceived once would not trade there again.

719. What should the character of a business man be ?

How She Managed It.

" What other persons call rascality I call shrewdness."
The remark was made by an old banker, notorious for his
selfishness and readiness to take advantage of all with
whom he dealt. He died a bankrupt, scorned and unla-
mented. The Providence *Journal* tells a story of a lady,—
so called,—which exhibits her as acting upon the banker's
code of morals:

"'Is my hat done?' inquired a cold-looking lady at a
Chicago millinery establishment one pleasant day this
week.

"'Yes, ma'am,' politely responded the shopkeeper. 'It
will be here in a moment.'

" An assistant soon brought up the bonnet, and while the
customer was duly inspecting it, the store proprietress ventured to inquire,—

"'How do you like it, ma'am?'

"'It is simply horrid,' was the reply.

"'But it is just as you ordered it,' pleaded the maker of
head-wear.

"'Yes, something as I ordered,' was the short and sneer-
ing answer.

"'I am really sorry, but——'

"'Well, never mind,' broke in the buyer, with set lips;
'what's the expense?'

"'A-b-o-u-t seven dollars, I guess,' said the shop-woman,
timidly.

" The money was paid over, and the bonnet ordered up
to the house, when the purchaser pranced out upon the
street, and immediately exclaimed to an accompanying lady
friend,—

"'Isn't it perfectly lovely?'

" ' Yes,' replied the friend, ' it's ravishing ! but how could you talk so to that woman ?'

" ' Talk so ?' exclaimed she of the new bonnet. ' Why, if I had let her know how much I liked the hat, that woman would certainly have charged me fifteen dollars; but now, you see, I've got it for seven !'

" The other woman said that she had never thought of that."

720. Relate the story of how she managed it.

721. Is it right for merchants to deceive their customers ?

722. Is it right for customers to deceive merchants ? Why ?

723. Was she a lady ?

See question No. 314.

724. Would a lady cheat a shop-keeper in the price of a hat ?

725. What is the difference between rascality and shrewdness ?

Rascality is dishonesty, hypocrisy, and meanness. Shrewdness means knowledge of business, smartness in knowing when and how and with whom to trade.

726. How may a business man be shrewd and at the same time not rascally ?

727. Was Mr. A. T. Stewart shrewd or rascally when he reproved his clerk ? Why ?

A Hole's Weight.

The following anecdote illustrates two very common facts, namely : a mean, suspicious man is apt to make a fool of himself, and the folly of a fool cannot stand against good sense.

Mr. ——, of a certain town in Vermont, is not distinguished for liberality. His ruling passion is a fear of being

P

cheated. The loss, whether real or fancied, of a few cents would give him more pain than the destruction of an entire navy.

He once bought a large cake of tallow at a country store, at ten cents a pound. On breaking it to pieces at home it was found to contain a large cavity.

This he considered a disclosure of cupidity and fraud. He drove furiously back to the store, entering in great excitement, bearing the cake of tallow, exclaiming, vehemently,—

"Here, you rascal, you have cheated me! Do you call that an honest cake of tallow? It is hollow, and there ain't near so much as there appeared to be. I want you to make it right."

"Certainly," replied the merchant; "I'll make it right. I didn't know the cake was hollow. You paid ten cents a pound. Now, Mr. ——, how much do you suppose the hole will weigh?"

728. Relate the story of the cake of tallow with a hole in it.

729. Which was the honest man in that transaction?

730. Was the man who bought the tallow shrewd or rascally?

731. Is it right to be suspicious of every one?

A business man should be prudent, but neither too suspicious nor too confiding.

732. What does the moral law say about weights and measures?

It says, "Ye shall do no unrighteousness,—

1st. In judgment.

2d. In mete-yard.

3d. In weights and measures.

4th. Just balances and weights shall ye have."

HIRING LABOR.

733. What kind of labor is hired for money?

All kinds,—manual, dextrous, and skilled.

734. What does the moral law say of the laborer's hire?

It says, "The laborer is worthy of his hire."

735. How many parties must there be to a hiring contract?

There must be two,—one to work and one to pay.

736. What is a contract?

See question No. 694.

737. In a contract for labor what is each party pledged to give the other?

One is pledged to give time and labor, the other is pledged to pay for the time and labor.

Wheeled Himself into Fortune.

At a meeting of the stockholders of a prominent railway corporation, recently held in Boston, there were present two gentlemen, both up in years, one, however, considerably the senior of the other. In talking of the old times gone by, the younger gentleman called the attention of his friends, and told a pleasant little story, which should be read with profit by every poor, industrious, and striving lad. We use his own language:

"Nearly half a century ago, gentlemen, I was put upon the world to make my living. I was stout, willing, and able, considering my tender years, and secured a place in a hardware store, to do all sorts of chores required. I was paid seventy-five dollars a year for my services. One day, after I had been at work three months or more, my friend there, Mr. B., who holds his age remarkably well, came into the store and bought a large bill of shovels and tongs, sad-irons and pans, buckets and scuttles, for he was to be married next day, and was supplying his household in advance, as was the groom's custom in those days. The articles were packed on the barrow and made a load sufficiently heavy for a young mule. But, more willing than able, I started off, proud that I could move such a mass on the wheelbarrow. I got on remarkably well till I struck the mud road, now Seventh Avenue, leading to my friend B.'s house. There I toiled and tugged, and tugged and toiled, and could not budge the load up the hill, the wheel going its full half-diameter in the mud every time I would try to propel forward. Finally, a good-natured Irishman, passing by with a dray, took my barrow, self and all, on his vehicle, and in consideration of my promise to pay him a ' bit,' landed me at the house.

" I counted the articles carefully as I delivered them, and with my empty barrow trudged my way back, whistling with glee over my triumph over difficulty. Some weeks after I paid the Irishman the ' bit,' and never got it back from my employers. But to the moral. A merchant had witnessed my struggles, and how zealously I labored to deliver that load of hardware; he even watched me to the house, and saw me count each piece as I landed it in the door-way. He sent for me the next day, asked my name, told me he had a reward for my industry and cheerfulness under difficulty, in the shape of a five-hundred-dollar clerkship in his establishment. I accepted, and now, after nearly half a century has passed, I look back and say, I wheeled myself into all I own, for that reward of perseverance was my grand stepping-stone to fortune."

The speaker was a very wealthy banker, a man of influence and position, and one universally respected for many good qualities of head and heart. Boys, take a moral from this story. You do not know how many eyes are upon you to discover whether you are sluggish and careless, or industrious and willing.

738. Relate how the young man wheeled himself into fortune.

739. What were the qualities that made that young man successful in business?

740. What was the secret of his promotion?

741. Should promotion ever be expected without faithful, honest, painstaking work? Why?

742. What are the terms used for the payment of laborers?

The teacher is paid tuition, the lawyer is paid fees, the minister receives a salary, the day-laborer receives hire, but the whole may be summed up in the word wages.

743. When should laborers be paid?

Always promptly according to the contract.

744. Why should laborers in the same class receive different rates of wages?

Because they have different degrees of skill and faithfulness.

745. Why are the wages of labor not the same at different times?

When laborers are scarce, wages are high; when laborers are plenty, wages are low.

746. Should employers take advantage of laborers, to make them work for less than their labor is worth?

747. Should laborers take advantage of their employers, and charge more for labor than it is worth?

748. What rule will apply to all such cases?

Repeat the Golden Rule.

P*

A Sensible Miner.

Mr. Charles B., a farmer of Washington County, Pennsylvania, was an Englishman, who emigrated, when a young man, to America for the purpose of making it his home. He was a coal-miner, and, for the purpose of finding employment, sought the coal mines of Western Pennsylvania. He was an uneducated man, but he was determined, by the help of his thrifty wife, to win the esteem and confidence of his neighbors by his industry and frugality. He rented a small piece of ground with his house, which he and his wife worked together as a garden and potato-patch when he was not employed in the mine. He was a man of good habits, wasting neither his time nor his money in bad company and foolish amusements. He could not afford to be idle, so, when by accident his arm was broken and he could not work in the mine, he went into a harvest-field and raked hay with one hand for twenty-five cents a day. When wages were high he saved his money; when wages were low, he thought it fortunate when he could pay expenses. Thus by habits of honest labor and economy he contrived to save enough money in the course of some years to buy him a fine farm, where he now lives in comfort, enjoying the confidence of his neighbors and the independence of a well-furnished home. It was a principle with him never to waste time when he could find work; never to quit work because he could not get the highest wages; never to drink spirits, and always to save his money. Of course, there were those who made fun of his hard work and economy, but now he is able to point to his home and his farm as the result of his shrewdness, while they have nothing to show for their years of misspent time and wasted money.

749. Relate the story of how Mr. B., the miner, made his farm.

750. Should every one be his own judge as to what wages he is willing to work for? Why?

751. When work is scarce and wages are low, is it best to take the low wages, or quit work and get no wages?

752. Has one person a right to prevent another from working for low wages? Why?

753. How may a person get the highest wages that are paid for his class of work?

By doing the best work.

754. What kind of laborers does everybody want?

Those that are the most honest, steady, and reliable.

HIRING AND RENTING PROPERTY.

755. What are meant by hiring and renting?

We hire the services of a person or an animal, and rent the use of houses or land.

756. How should we use a hired horse or a rented house?

Use them with the same care we would our own.

757. Should we overwork a hired horse?

No; it would be cruelty to the horse and injustice to its owner.

BORROWING.

758. What is meant by borrowing?

It is an agreement to take goods or money from another, with the promise of returning the same thing, or something of the same kind of equal amount or value, at a given time.

759. What are those two parties called?

The borrower and the lender.

The Borrowed Tiger.

Cardinal Alberoni had a large quantity of silver-plate,
and among other articles he possessed various salt-cellars,
wrought in the form of different animals.   A friend of
his Eminence borrowed a salt-cellar made in the shape of
a tiger, but forgot to return it for some time.   At length,
after the lapse of six or seven months, he sent it back,
requesting at the same time the loan of another in the
shape of a tortoise.   The cardinal desired to see the person
who had brought the message.   " You are sent," said he,
" by the Signor to borrow one of my salt-cellars ?"

" Yes, your Eminence ; I am his steward."

" You will be good enough to tell your master that I lent
him one in the form of a tiger, which is one of the swiftest
of the animals on the earth, and it has been more than six
months in returning : were I to lend him the tortoise, which
is the slowest of animals, I fear it would never return."

760. Relate the story of the borrowed tiger.

761. What is the duty in borrowing?

The duty of the borrower is to fulfil exactly the terms
of the agreement.

762. What is the danger in borrowing?

There is danger that borrowers may neglect or forget to
return the articles in good order and at the right time.

763. What may borrowers lose by their neglect?

They may lose their good name for honesty, carefulness,
and truthfulness.

BORROWING BOOKS.

764. Is it safe to borrow books ?

Many people do not like to lend books.   They are so

easily injured that it is often a trial of friendship to have them soiled or torn.

765. What special care should be taken by the borrower of books?

Books should be very carefully used, and promptly returned to the lender after they have been read.

766. Is it right for a person who has borrowed a book to lend it?

Not without the owner's consent.

The two following questions need not be answered aloud:

767. Are you a borrower?

768. Do you always comply with the terms of your contract?

769. A boy borrows a knife, and accidentally breaks it; what should he do? Why?

BORROWING MONEY.

770. Why do persons borrow money?

Persons borrow money to invest in trade, that they may realize a profit on it.

771. What is meant by interest?

It is money paid for the use of borrowed money.

772. What rule should always govern the borrower and lender of money?

773. Is it right for the money-lender to ask a reasonable interest for the loan of money?

Yes, for the same reason that it is right to ask hire for the use of a horse, or rent for the use of a house.

774. How may a person easily lose credit for honesty?

By borrowing small sums of money and neglecting to pay according to promise.

775. What is meant by usury?

It means an illegal or exorbitant rate of interest.

776. Should a lender take advantage of the necessities of the borrower to exact an excessive rate of interest ?

No more than he should in ordinary times to exact an excessive price for wheat.

True Pride.

A young man named Parks, from Worcester, entered the store of the Lawrences, in Boston, and found Amos in the office. He represented himself as having just commenced business, and desired to purchase a lot of goods. He had recommendations as to character from several influential citizens of Worcester, but none touching his business standing or capacity. The merchant listened to his story, and at its close shook his head.

"I have no doubt," he said, kindly, "that you have full faith in your ability to promptly meet the obligations you would now assume, but I have no knowledge of your tact or capacity, and, as you are just launching out on the sea of business, I should be doing you a great injustice to allow you to contract a debt which I did not feel assured you could pay at the proper time."

But Mr. Lawrence liked the appearance of the young man, and finally told him that he would let him have what goods he could pay for at the cost of manufacture,—about ten per cent. less than the regular wholesale price. The bill was made out and paid, and the clerk asked where the goods should be sent.

"I will take them myself," said the purchaser.

"You will find them rather heavy," suggested the clerk, smiling.

"Never mind ; I am strong, and the stage-office is not far away ; and, besides, I have nothing else to occupy my time."

" But," said the clerk, expostulating, " it is hardly in keeping with your position to be shouldering such ponderous bundles through the city."

" There you mistake," replied the young man, with simple candor. " My position just now is one in which I must help myself, if I would be helped at all. I am not ashamed to carry anything which I honestly possess, nor am I ashamed of the strength which enables me to bear this heavy burden."

Thus speaking, he shouldered a large bundle, and had turned towards the outer door, when Mr. Lawrence, who from his office had overheard the conversation, called him back.

" Mr. Parks, I have concluded to let you have what goods you want on time. Select at your pleasure."

The young man was surprised.

" You have the true pride for a successful merchant, sir," pursued Mr. Lawrence, " and I shall be much disappointed if you do not prosper."

Amos Lawrence was not disappointed. Within fifteen years from that time Mr. Parks was one of the most enterprising and successful merchants in Boston.

777. Relate the story of Mr. Parks, who got goods on credit.

778. What is meant by getting goods on time?

The merchant lets the customer have goods to be paid for at a future time.

779. What is meant by losing credit?

A man loses credit when people believe he is either unable or unwilling to pay his debts.

780. What reason had Mr. Lawrence for refusing to sell the young man goods on time?

781. Why did he change his mind?

782. What was "the true pride of a successful merchant"?

783. How did Mr. Parks use his credit, and what was the result?

COVETOUSNESS.

784. What is meant by covetousness?

An undue desire to acquire property.

785. What does the moral law say about covetousness?

It says, "Thou shalt not covet thy neighbor's house . . . nor anything that is thy neighbor's."

786. Why is covetousness immoral?

Because an improper desire to get property may lead to the use of very improper means.

787. What are some of the sins to which covetousness leads?

It leads to lying, cheating, gambling, and stealing.

Covetousness Punished.

M. Dugar, provost of the merchants in the city of Lyons, was a man remarkable for the strict and impartial administration of justice. The bakers flattered themselves that they could prevail upon him to be their friend at the expense of the public. They waited upon him in a body, and begged leave to raise the price of bread. He told them that he would examine their petition, and give them an answer very soon; before they left the room they contrived slyly to drop a purse of two hundred *louis d'or* on the table. They soon called upon the magistrate for an answer, not in the least doubting but the money had effectually pleaded their cause.

"Gentlemen," said M. Dugar, "I have weighed your

reasons in the balance of justice, and I find them light. I do not think the people ought to suffer under a pretence of the dearness of corn, which I know to be ill-founded. As to the purse of money which you left with me, I am certain that I have made such a generous and noble use of it as you yourselves intended; I have distributed it among the poor objects of charity in our hospitals. As you are *opulent enough* to make such *large donations,* I cannot possibly think that you can incur any loss in your business, and I therefore shall continue the price of bread as it was before I received your petition."

788. Relate the story of covetousness punished.

789. What did the bakers' covetousness lead them to attempt?

They tried to bribe a public officer.

790. How did the provost punish them for their crime?

791. Is there anything we may covet without injury to ourselves or our neighbor?

We may covet purity, gentleness, kindness, and charity, and the good fruits of an honest life.

792. Why may these virtues be coveted?

LOST PROPERTY.

Honesty the Best Policy.

A clergyman in England, with a large family and a small salary, once found a purse of gold, which he carried home; and being distressed for the want of money was almost persuaded to use some of it, but he refrained, alleging that " Honesty is the best policy," and that it was his duty to try to find the owner. This he soon did, but the owner only gave him thanks as his reward, which exposed the good man to some reproaches from his family. A few months afterward, however, the same gentleman sent for

Q

the clergyman to dinner, and presented him a church with a salary of three hundred pounds a year and fifty pounds for present use. He went home to his family with joy, and they readily agreed with him that in the end " Honesty is the best policy."

793. Relate the story of the restored purse.

794. Should we ask any reward for restoring a lost purse?

We have no right to demand pay for being honest.

795. If the finder of property has been put to cost and trouble in taking care of it, or in advertising it, what may he demand?

The owner should pay all reasonable expenses for getting back his property.

796. Did the clergyman do wrong to accept a present from the owner upon the return of his purse?

797. If the owner cannot be found, who shall get the property?

The finder has the next best right to it.

798. What should be done with articles lost and found at school?

799. How may lost articles at school be advertised?

800. What should the finder do with property he has found?

801. What temptation is offered the finder of property?

802. If the finder of property conceals it, what crime does he commit?

WILD GAME.

803. If a man catches fish in the stream and kills squirrels in the woods, to whom do they belong?

They belong to those who capture them, because before they were taken they had no owner.

804. Where may we fish and hunt game?

Wherever the law permits and the land-owners make no objection.

805. If the owner of the land objects, have we a right to go upon his land to hunt or fish?

Certainly not.

806. May you take fish from your neighbor's pond without his permission? Why?

807. What is the difference in the ownership of the fish in a public stream and those in a private pond?

GAMBLING.

808. What is meant by gambling?

1st. It is playing at games of skill or chance for money or other valuables.

2d. Or it is betting for money or other property.

809. What is a gambler?

It is a person who practises gaming.

810. Why is gambling wrong?

1st. It is the result of covetousness, which tries to obtain money or other valuables without work.

2d. Nothing is given in exchange for money won in gambling.

3d. Because it leads to quarrelling and often to murder.

811. What is the character of gamblers generally?

They are generally cheats and hypocrites.

812. To what habits does gambling lead?

To habits of idleness, dishonesty, and crime.

An Eye for a Pin.

Two boys named Abel and Asa were at the same school in New York, each about ten years old, not brothers, but school-mates and class-mates. Both of them had irritable tempers, and had been taught to think they must resent injuries and defend their rights at all hazards. Playing *pin* was a favorite amusement in the school. They played in this way : two boys would take a hat and set it down between them ; then each boy would lay a pin on top of the crown, and then knock it,—first one, and then the other. The one that could knock the pins so that they would lie across each other had them both. During recess one day Abel and Asa were playing pin. They knocked the pins about some time. Both became much excited in the game. Finally, Abel knocked the pins so that, as he said, one lay across the point of the other. Asa denied it ; Abel declared they did, and snatched up both pins. Asa's anger flashed in a moment, and he struck Abel in the face. This excited Abel's wrath. They began to fight, the other boys clustering around, not to part them, but to urge them on. Some cried, "Hit him, Abel !" and some, "Give it to him, Asa !" thus stimulating them to quarrel. The boys seized each other, and finally came tumbling to the ground, Abel on top. Then Abel, in his fury, went to beating Asa in his face till the blood spouted from his nose and mouth and till Asa lay like one dead. Then the boys pulled Abel off. But Asa could not get up. The boys began to be alarmed ; they were afraid Abel had killed him. The teacher was called. He carried Asa in, washed the blood from his face, and recovered him from his stupor. He examined his face and head, and found them bruised in a shocking manner. One of his eyes was so hurt and swollen he could not open it. And from that time the sight of it grew more and more dim, till it went out in total darkness. So Asa lost an eye, and Abel put it out, merely for a pin !

813. Relate the story of an eye for a pin.
814. Is playing for pins gambling ?
See question No. 808.

815. If it be wrong to gamble for dollars, is it right to gamble for cents? Why?

816. If it be wrong to gamble for money, is it right to gamble for marbles, tops, or pins?

817. Why is it wrong to gamble for marbles or pins?

The habit of gambling for little things may lead to the habit of gambling for money.

818. Is it right to play games of skill and chance when we do not gamble?

Certainly; we may play for amusement and recreation if we do not gamble.

819. Are all games alike innocent?

There is a difference; some offer greater temptations to gambling than others.

For a further discussion of this subject, see the chapter on the Practical Application of Politeness in Play.

THE LOTTERY.

820. What is a lottery?

A lottery is a scheme of prizes and blanks which are drawn by lot, upon the payment of a sum of money for a ticket.

821. What is a raffle?

A raffle is a kind of lottery, in which the players pay for a chance to win a prize by the throwing of dice, or by shooting at a mark.

Lottery and Suicide.

In 1833 an adventurer in lotteries committed suicide in the city of Boston by drowning himself. He was in the employment of one of the most respectable houses in the city, highly esteemed and respected by the members of it, and in the receipt of a liberal salary. About a year before he had the misfortune to draw a prize in the lottery, and

Q*

from that moment his ruin was sealed. The regular earnings of honest industry were no longer enough for him,—visions of splendid prizes were continually flitting before his eyes, and he plunged at once into the intoxicating excitement of lotteries. He soon became deeply involved, and his access to the funds of the firm held out to him a temptation which he could not resist. He appropriated to himself considerable sums from time to time, continually deluded by the hope that a turn of the wheel would give him the means of replacing them. But that turn never came; fortune gave him but one smile, and that was a fatal one. He saw that detection would soon come, and that the punishment and the shame of a felon would succeed to the consideration and respect he had always enjoyed, and he had not courage to wait the moment of disclosure. He sought refuge in death, and added to his other sins the horrible act of self-murder. He left a memorandum, which contained an account of the circumstances that made life intolerable to him.

822. Relate the story of the lottery and suicide.

823. What were the successive wrong steps in the young man's course?

824. What was the last step he took, and his reason for taking it?

825. What effect have lotteries upon the people who gamble at them?

It makes them idle, superstitious, and restless, for they live in the hope that their lucky number will give them a prize without the trouble of working for it.

CHURCH-FAIR LOTTERIES.

826. Is a lottery for a church better than any other lottery?

827. Why is a church-fair raffle better than any other?

828. Is the habit of gambling learned at a church fair different from the same habit learned in a gambling-saloon?

829. Does the cause for which people gamble sanctify the gambling? Why?

830. Is it right to arouse the covetousness of our neighbor by selling him a lottery ticket? Why?

831. Is it the desire of doing good, or the hope of drawing a prize that leads people to take chances at church-festival lotteries?

The following questions need not be answered aloud:

832. Do you gamble with pins and marbles?

833. Do you sell tickets for church-fair raffles, and thus tempt others to gamble?

834. Do you expect to grow up with gambling habits? Why?

835. Are you brighter, smarter, or better able to stand the temptations of covetousness than others who have been ruined by this vice?

STEALING.

836. What is meant by stealing?

Stealing is the taking and carrying away of the goods of another without his knowledge and consent.

837. What desire leads people to steal?

Covetousness leads people to take what does not belong to them.

838. What is he called who steals?

839. How much or how little should one steal to be a thief? Why?

840. What does the moral law say about stealing?

It says, " Thou shalt not steal."

841. What does that mean?

It means thou shalt not take *anything* from *anybody* without his knowledge and consent.

842. May we not take fruit from an orchard, or melons from a field, in fun? Why?

843. Is there any fun in stealing? To whom?

844. What shall we call the taking of an apple from a wagon, or a slate-pencil from a desk?

845. Does the crime of stealing depend upon the value of the thing taken?

846. How may habits of stealing be formed?

An Honest Boy.

During a terrible conflagration in Virginia City, while the fire was raging, and thousands of houses were going to destruction on the tempest of flame, a boy presented himself at the house of W. H. Smith, superintendent of the Belcher, and asked what he could do to render them assistance. The servant-girl handed him a small box containing jewels and other valuables to the amount of six thousand dollars, requesting him to carry it to Wells, Fargo & Co.'s office.

He did so, and, with a business tact far beyond his years, demanded a receipt therefor. This was refused. He was told the vault was closed, but that they would put the box with other things. He told them the box belonged to Mr. Smith, and if they would not give him a receipt therefor, he would take charge of it himself.

The fire passed. The home of Mr. Smith, went with the other buildings, and he was compelled to find accommodations elsewhere. He thus missed the boy, and the boy him. He advertised for the boy, and as soon as the lad knew where to find him he returned the box, not a jewel missing.

One does not know which to admire most, his honesty

or the keen business tact which told him that a receipt was necessary to prove he had been faithful to his trust.

847. Relate the story of the honest boy.

848. Suppose the boy had hid the jewel-box and said nothing, what then?

849. Would he probably have been as happy to have retained the box, or to return it as he did? Why?

850. What effect would the return of the box have had upon the boy's conscience? Why?

851. What effect would the knowledge of the fact by others have upon the reputation of the boy?

The moral law says, " A good name is rather to be chosen than great riches."

852. How shall we gain a good name for honesty?

By being strictly honest in little things as well as in great matters.

The Incorruptible Duke.

The Duke of Wellington was a distinguished example of dogged British fidelity. It has been said of him that he just escaped being " stupid," but his stupidity consisted mainly in his peculiar blindness to the " advantages" of doing wrong. When tempted to treachery or inveigled into any crooked dealing he " couldn't see it."

When Lord Wellington was commander of an army in India, a certain rich man offered him five hundred thousand dollars for some secret information on a very important question. Wellington looked thoughtfully a few moments, as if he was weighing the temptation. But he was not. He was only considering the best way to answer his tempter. At length he said,—

" It appears that you can keep a secret, sir?"

" Certainly," replied the man, feeling sure he had gained his point.

"So can I," rejoined Wellington. " Good-morning, sir."
And the man went away with a chop-fallen air.

853. Relate the story of the incorruptible duke.

854. What is the difference between getting money as a bribe and stealing?

855. Could the man who would offer a bribe be trusted with an important secret?

A rascal who would bribe a person would betray him if he thought it to his interest to do so. A liar or a thief cannot be safely trusted.

The following three questions need not be answered aloud:

856. Do you try in all things to be perfectly honest?

857. Are you forming habits of strict honesty in all your transactions at home and at school?

858. Can you be trusted by everybody as entirely worthy of confidence?

PUBLIC PROPERTY.

859. What is the property called that belongs to the town, the city, or to the State?

It is called public property, and belongs to the people.

860. Name some buildings that are public property.

The bridge, the court-house, the school-house, etc.

861. Why are these buildings said to be public property?

Because they were built by the taxes collected from the people.

862. Who have the right to use these buildings?

They are used by and for the people.

863. Can public property be converted to private uses?

It may be, under proper restrictions.

864. What are the restrictions?

1st. That the private use does not interfere with the public use.

2d. That the permission be secured from the proper officers who are authorized to give it.

865. As every citizen has an interest in the public property, has any citizen, therefore, a right to injure or destroy it?

No one has a right to injure or destroy anything that does not wholly belong to himself.

866. Has a man a right to destroy his own property?

Yes, as long as the destruction does no harm to his neighbors or to society.

867. What would be your impression of a family whose house is defaced and dirty?

868. What should you think of a school whose rooms are dirty, whose seats and desks are defaced, whose doors and walls are abused?

869. If a family is judged by the neatness and cleanliness of the home, is it fair to judge of the good taste of the teacher and pupils from the condition of the school-house?

870. Who should have the credit or discredit of a neat, clean, well-kept school or its opposite?

The following five questions need not be answered aloud:

871. Do you mark the walls, deface the doors, and cut the furniture of your home? Why?

872. Is your name scribbled on the school-house premises? Why?

873. Have you ever defaced the school-house by marking or whittling? Why?

874. Is your desk defaced by cutting or marking?

875. Can you by your words and example prevent such abuse of the school property?

PRACTICAL APPLICATION OF THE PRINCIPLES OF POLITENESS AT HOME.

876. What is your duty to your family at home?

It is the duty of every member of the family to try to make the rest happy.

877. What rule should govern each member of the family?

" Whatsoever ye would that men should do to you, do ye even so to them."

878. How do the members of a family stand to each other?

As superiors, equals, and inferiors.

879. What are the rights of each member?

Each should be treated according to his station, with kindness and politeness.

880. When only should each one claim his rights?

Only when he has faithfully done his duty.

RISING IN THE MORNING.

881. What should we do when called in the morning?

Rise promptly, so that no one be kept waiting on our account.

882. What are the first duties of the morning?

To dress promptly, wash the face and hands, and comb or brush the hair.

883. How should we leave the sleeping-room?

Everything should be left in good order.

884. How should the wash-stand be left?

The water in the basin should be emptied, and the towels properly hung up.

885. How should we keep each room?

1st. There should be a place for everything, and everything should be kept in its place.

2d. Everything should be kept neat and clean.

3d. Always leave the room in good order.

ENTERING ROOMS.

886. How shall we enter a private room?

Always knock before entering a private room when we are not expected.

887. How shall we enter an office or other public place?

Always enter without knocking.

888. Of what use are the scraper and mat at the door?

889. How shall we use the door on entering or leaving a room?

1st. If the season requires it, we should always close the door.

2d. The door should be closed gently, and not slammed.

890. How shall we receive a visitor?

1st. Answer the knock or ring at the door promptly.

2d. Invite the visitor in, who will state the object of the visit.

3d. If on an errand, offer the visitor a seat while you carry the message.

4th. If on a visit, treat the visitor with politeness, asking him or her into the room for visitors.

891. Returning from school, what does good breeding require?

1st. The boys will always remove their hats when entering the house.

2d. Hang up all wraps, hats, and bonnets.

3d. Put by books, umbrellas, overshoes, in their proper places.

892. When shall the boys whistle and the girls scream?

Perhaps for the comfort of the other members of the

house they had better not whistle or scream. If they must do so, let them go to the barn.

893. If any one whistles as a signal to come out of the house, what should we do?

We should decline such an invitation and send the dog.

894. Is it polite to sneak about a house and whistle for some one to come out?

It would be more manly and polite to knock or ring at the door and inquire for the person wanted.

895. How should we arrange our time at home?

We should have regular times for work, for study, and for play.

896. If attending school, when should we attend social parties and merry-makings?

Better not go to such affairs if they would interfere with school.

897. If about equal in age, what should govern brothers and sisters in going to places of amusement and in visiting?

They should go, if possible, together.

898. What kind of manners should we practise at home?

We should always practise at home what it would be polite to practise away from home.

HOME ENGAGEMENTS.

899. How should engagements be kept?

Everybody should be punctual to an engagement.

A Royal Reproof.

When Queen Victoria was about thirty years younger than she is now, she was inclined to be very exact in the way of business, and more especially in the way of promptness to appointed times and places. Seven years a queen, four years a wife, and three years a mother, she felt, probably, a more weighty dignity resting upon her than she has felt since. And yet, no crust of dignity or royal station could ever entirely shut out her innate goodness of heart.

At the time of which we speak, the Duchess of Sutherland held the office of mistress of the robes of the British queen, and on public occasions her position was very near her royal person, and deemed of great importance. A day and an hour had been appointed for a certain public ceremony in which the queen was to take part.

The hour had arrived, and of all the court the duchess alone was absent, and her absence retarded the departure. The queen gave vent more than once to her impatience, and at length, as she was about to enter the carriage without her first lady of honor, the duchess, in breathless haste, made her appearance, stammering some faint words of excuse.

"My dear duchess," said the queen, smiling, "I think you must have a bad watch."

And as she thus spoke, she unloosed from her neck the chain of a magnificent watch she herself wore, and passed it around the neck of Lady Sutherland.

Though given as a present, the lesson conveyed with it made a deep impression. The proud duchess changed color, and a tear, which she could not repress, fell upon her cheek. On the next day she tendered her resignation, but it was not accepted. It is said that ever afterwards she was, if anything, more punctual than the queen herself.

900. Relate the story of the royal reproof.

901. Why should the members of a family be punctual?

While we may waste our own time, we have no right to waste the time of our neighbor.

902. What is the effect on the character of those who are not punctual?

People who fail to make good their promises soon lose their good name for truthfulness.

PRACTICAL APPLICATION OF THE PRINCIPLES OF POLITENESS AT THE TABLE.

903. May we be tardy in coming to our meals?

Nothing disturbs the pleasure of a family so much as irregularity at meals.

904. Why is tardiness at meals in a private family so annoying?

The tardiness of one interferes with all; any delay disturbs the business order of the whole house.

905. What effect has tardiness on the servants?

It interferes with their work. We have no right unnecessarily or carelessly to cause them trouble even though they are paid for their services.

906. How shall we treat servants?

See question 158.

907. How shall we sit at table?

See question No. 235.

908. What should be the dress at meals?

1st. Our dress should correspond with that of the company.

2d. It should not offend by not being clean.

3d. Men and boys should not come to table in their shirt-sleeves.

909. Why should not men and boys come to table in their shirt-sleeves?

It may be that they have been overheated, and the odor of perspiration would be particularly disagreeable at table.

910. How should the elbows be held at table?

They should not be rested upon the table, but held near the sides, so as not to interfere with our neighbors.

911. What shall be done with the hands?

1st. When not using the knife, fork, or spoon the hands should rest upon the napkin in the lap.

2d. The hands should never scratch or rub the head or face during meals.

912. How shall we behave if we are hungry?

It is in very bad taste to appear greedy or hungry.

913. How shall guests be seated at table?

The lady of the house should always arrange her guests, and the seat of honor should be given to the stranger or to the eldest.

914. Who should be helped first at table?

The strangers and the elders first; the ladies before the gentlemen, and the young people last.

915. How shall we act if we do not like some of the dishes?

It is very impolite to appear dainty at the table, but if we have a distaste for any dish we need not eat it.

916. When shall the guests begin to eat?

Not until all are helped. If there are several courses, the guests should begin each course together.

917. May we talk when we eat?

Care should be taken not to talk or drink when we are eating, lest we be set coughing.

918. If it be necessary to cough at table, what should we do?

We should turn the head from the table and cover the mouth with the hand or with the napkin.

919. Is it polite to spit or to blow the nose at table?

It is very rude to spit or to blow the nose. If it be necessary to do either, we had better quietly leave the table.

R*

KNIFE, FORK, AND SPOON.

920. How shall we use our knife, fork, and spoon?

1st. The knife is to be used for cutting the food, while the fork and the spoon are used to convey the food to the mouth.

2d. We should not use our own knife or spoon to take butter or sauce from the common dish. We should use the butter-knife and the table-spoon.

TABLE-CLOTH AND NAPKIN.

921. How should the napkin be used?

The napkin should be used to wipe the mouth and the finger-tips. If there be no napkin, the handkerchief should be used. The napkin should not be used as a handkerchief to wipe perspiration from the face.

922. How should the table-cloth be used?

Great care should be taken not to soil it, nor should it ever be used as a napkin to wipe the fingers.

923. At the close of the meal what shall we do with the napkin?

1st. Fold it neatly, and put it in the napkin-ring to be used again.

2d. If we do not expect to use it again, as at a hotel, lay it carefully beside the plate.

CONVERSATION AT TABLE.

924. What subjects of conversation should be introduced at the table?

Only such subjects should be spoken of as are interesting to the company. But of this the elders must be the judge.

925. What care should be taken in the conversation?

1st. We should be careful not to allude to anything that may excite unpleasant emotions or disgust.

2d. The younger members of the company should be very modest, and not intrude their opinions unless they are asked.

926. When asked for an opinion, how should it be given ?

Kindly, politely, and respectfully.

927. What should young folks particularly avoid ?

They should never make themselves the subjects of remark, or the heroes of their own story.

THE SERVANTS.

928. Should any accident happen at table, how should we treat it ?

We should not take notice of it in such a way as to hurt one's feelings.

929. How may we call the servant ?

A gentle tapping upon the cup with the spoon will attract the attention of the servant.

930. How shall we treat the servants at table ?

Always treat them politely. It is very rude to reprove a servant in presence of company.

931. How shall we ask to be helped ?

Always say, " Will you please help me ——?" and say it distinctly, so as not to be misunderstood.

932. How shall we acknowledge attentions at table ?

Always with a pleasant smile and a kind " I thank you."

933. How shall we use the cup and saucer ?

We should drink from the cup, and not from the saucer.

934. How may we show our wish to have our plates changed ?

Place the knife and fork side by side on the plate, and the servant will see that the plate is to be changed.

935. What assistance shall we render at the table ?

At a hotel it is not expected that anybody will render assistance at table except the servants, but among friends at a private table each guest should see that all the rest are provided for.

LEAVING THE TABLE.

936. When shall we leave the table?

It is impolite to leave the table until all are done eating. If one must leave, he should ask the company to excuse him.

937. Should we take nuts or fruit with us when we leave the table?

It is very rude to take anything from the table unless we first ask permission of the lady who presides at the table.

938. Should gentlemen smoke after meals in a private house?

They had better not, unless they are invited to do so. It may be very disagreeable to the household.

PRACTICAL APPLICATION OF THE PRINCIPLES OF POLITENESS ON THE STREET.

STREET DRESS.

939. How should people dress to walk upon the street?

1st. The dress should not be such as to attract undue notice upon the street.

2d. It should always be suited to the season.

3d. The immodesty of women may be inferred if they do not regard the proprieties of dress on the street.

940. How should persons, particularly boys and girls, behave on the street?

1st. They should never appear anxious to attract public notice by rudeness to each other.

2d. They should never talk or laugh in such a manner as would lead strangers to suppose they wished to be observed.

PASSING ON THE STREET.

941. How should we pass each other on the street and sidewalk ?

1st. Each should pass to the right.

2d. Each should give the other the half of the way.

942. How shall a person pass when going in the same direction ?

The one wishing to pass should, if possible, go to the left.

943. How shall a lady and gentleman walk together upon the pavement ?

On the street people meet and pass to the right. If the lady walks on the right of the gentleman in a crowded street, she will be less likely to be jostled than if she walked on his left.

944. In crossing a muddy street which should go first, the lady or the gentleman ?

The gentleman should go first, for the same reason that he should go first up a flight of stairs.

945. When a lady and gentleman meet upon the street, which shall speak first ?

The lady is always expected to speak first.

946. If the lady is veiled should the gentleman recognize her ?

Unless she removes her veil she shows she does not wish to be recognized. Being veiled, the gentleman might not recognize her if he wished.

947. If young people meet their superiors, who should speak first ?

The superiors should always speak first, and the young people should not speak till they are addressed.

948. How should a boy return the politeness of a lady or gentleman who speaks to him on the street?

He should return the compliment by taking off his hat.

949. If intimate friends should meet on the street, or in any public place, should they embrace and kiss each other?

It is not considered in good taste for friends to appear affectionate in public.

950. Should a gentleman smoke when walking in public with a lady?

It does not appear respectful to the lady, even if it is done with her consent.

951. Is it polite for men and boys to stand upon the streets to make comments on those who pass?

No gentleman could be guilty of such rudeness.

952. How should we always treat strangers who are seeking information on the street?

A civil question always demands a civil answer.

Only a Broken Hoop.

It was a little thing, so worthless that it had been thrown in the street, yet it did a deed of violence and blood,—it was but a broken iron hoop. Some one wished to get rid of it, and so it rested quietly in a public street, where thousands of horses and men and women pass. A New York paper tells the rest of the story:

Mr. William McGuire, a wealthy builder of Brooklyn, was riding in a light top buggy with his son, behind a spirited horse. The front wheel of the buggy passed over a broken hoop, which entangled itself in the spokes, leaving one end projecting from the wheel.

As the wheel revolved, this projecting point, ragged and sharp, struck the horse in the flank, and at every revolution of the wheel repeated the blow. The horse bounded forward, and sped over the pavement.

As the iron inflicted its repeated stings, the horse plunged in a mad gallop. Mr. McGuire, who had tried to check him, suddenly grew pale and said to his son, " Charlie, we're gone !"

The wheels, catching in a car track, upset the carriage in an instant. Mr. McGuire was thrown a complete somersault, alighting on his head and shoulders. His son, who clung to the reins, was thrown out on his hip.

Mr. McGuire's skull was fractured and his collar-bone broken. He was carried home in an ambulance. He died.

It was a thoughtless act, the throwing of that hoop into a public street, and the evils of this world result largely from the want of consideration.

953. Relate the story of the broken hoop.

954. Have we a right to throw rubbish on the streets or in the road ? Why ?

955. Is it a sufficient excuse, when we throw broken glass, or orange-peel, or apple-parings upon the sidewalk, to say, " I did not think" ? Why ?

956. Who is responsible for accidents resulting from such carelessness ?

SPORTS ON THE STREETS.

957. Is it right to make the sidewalk a sliding-place in winter ?

958. If an old person should fall and break a leg or an arm on the sliding-place, who would be responsible?

959. What principle should govern right-minded boys

as to the throwing of stones, snow-balls, or fire-crackers in the streets?

960. Are the rolling of hoops, the playing of ball, the flying of kites, and other such amusements, proper in the streets, where people and horses are passing? Why?

961. Whose property is a handbill or poster?

962. Is it right to disturb posters, handbills, finger-boards, and other such signs that are intended to give information to the public? Why?

963. Is it proper to write our own or others' names in public places?

Modest, well-bred people never deface property in that way, or court notoriety by putting themselves before the public in that way.

How Friendship was Broken.

Two young ladies of the town of W., in Pennsylvania, were life-long friends. They had grown up together as neighbors and school-mates, and were inseparable as companions. One was somewhat singular in appearance, having a short neck and very broad, square shoulders, that gave an impression of physical deformity. But what she lacked in physical grace was more than made up by the sweetness of her temper and the gentleness of her disposition. She was kind and loving to every one, but very sensitive as to her physical defects.

There was at the academy a young man who possessed some skill as an artist. He had observed the peculiarity of Miss N., and with a cruel desire for fun at the expense of an unoffending lady, who could not resent the insult, he drew a caricature of her upon the inside walls of an unoccupied building. It soon became noised around that a funny caricature of Miss N. had been placed there. Drawn by curiosity, the place was visited by Miss M. in company with another and older woman, but it did not occur to either of them that they had any office of friendship to perform in the matter.

Shortly after Miss N., having heard that she had been made the subject of a cruel jest, called upon her friend, and told her that she had learned there was a caricature in the house referred to which was as disgraceful as it was cruel.

"Yes," said Miss M., "Mrs. H. and I saw it there."

"And did you not rub it out?" said Miss N.

"Why, no," said Miss M.; "we never thought of that."

"Then I cannot feel that you are my friend."

From that time the friendship was broken.

964. Relate the story of how friendship was broken.

965. What should we do if we should see our own or our friends' names scribbled in a public place?

966. What motive should govern us in everything we do on the public streets or in public places?

We should act like well-bred people, giving to every one every right we claim for ourselves, interfering with nobody, offending nobody.

PRACTICAL APPLICATION OF THE PRINCIPLES OF POLITENESS AT CHURCH.

967. For what purpose are churches built?

They are built to promote the worship of God.

968. Do all people agree in their worship of God?

No. There is a great difference among people in religious belief and worship.

969. Why are there so many kinds of churches?

8

Those who think alike about God worship together in their own church.

970. Have we a right to compel others to think and worship God as we do?

No. Every one has a right to worship God in the way he thinks best.

971. How should persons behave in their own church?

Well-bred people always show respect for God's house and his worship.

972. How should persons behave who visit strange churches?

1st. They should always respect the rights and feelings of those who worship there.

2d. They should join in the worship if in accordance with their belief.

973. How do impolite, irreverent people sometimes disturb religious services?

1st. By coming in late.

2d. By appearing restless and inattentive.

3d. By talking, laughing, and writing notes to each other.

974. If we do not believe as the people of the church do, have we a right to disturb them?

As we are under no obligations to attend, the least we can do is to behave properly while there.

Irreverence Rebuked.

It is both wicked and silly to behave irreverently in church. A student of the University of Cambridge, England, was once sharply reminded of this truth. Shortly after Rev. Robert Robinson, noted in his day as a preacher and sayer of *good things,* was settled over the Baptist church in that town, a bet was made by a party of students. One of them wagered that he would stand on the pulpit-stairs with a large ear-trumpet in his hand, and remain there till the end of the service. Accordingly, one Sunday he mounted the stairs, put the trumpet to his ear, and gravely played the part of a deaf-mute. His friends, scattered through the church, tittered at the hoax. The congregation were indignant, but the preacher seemed unmoved. The sermon was on the mercy of God, and the preacher soon gave a practical illustration of it, saying,—

" Not only, my Christian friends, does the mercy of God extend to the most enormous of criminals, so that none, however guilty, may not, if duly penitent, be partakers of the divine grace, but also there are none so low, so mean, so worthless as not to be objects of God's fatherly solicitude and care. Indeed, I do hope that it may one day be extended to"—then, leaning over the pulpit, he stretched out his arm, and, placing it on the student's head, finished his sentence—" to this silly boy !"

The wager was lost, for the trumpet fell, and the abashed student retired.

975. Relate how irreverence was rebuked.

976. What reason could be given by the young man for such behavior ? Was it witty or smart ?

977. How should we treat strangers at church ?

1st. We should see that they are invited to a comfortable seat.

2d. We should offer them whatever books are necessary for them to unite in the service.

978. How should we act when visiting a strange church ?

1st. We should take the seat offered us.

2d. We should thank those who are polite to us.

3d. We should never disturb the congregation by leaving before the services are ended.

4th. We should never spit upon the floors.

5th. When the services are ended, we should not show unbecoming haste in getting away.

6th. We should not stand around the door after the services are ended and gaze upon the congregation as they leave the church.

The following questions need not be answered aloud:

979. Do you always behave respectfully in church?

980. Do you sit where you can be readily seen, or do you sneak back to escape observation?

981. Do you run in and out during the services, and disturb the congregation?

982. Is your conduct in church always such as to meet the approval of good people?

PRACTICAL APPLICATION OF THE PRINCIPLES OF POLITENESS AT PLAY.

983. What things is it desirable that children should know about play?

They should know,—

1st. When to play.

2d. What to play.

3d. With whom to play; and

4th. How to play.

984. *When* should children play?

1st. When play interferes with no duty at home.

2d. When it interferes with no duty at school.

3d. At suitable hours.

4th. At regular times.

5th. When it is agreeable to parents or guardians.

985. *What* should children play?

1st. Such games or plays as are approved by our parents.

2d. Such as are approved generally by good people.

3d. Such as will not endanger health.

4th. Such as will not endanger others.

5th. Such as will not interfere with others' rights.

6th. Such as will not lead into bad places or bad company.

7th. Such as will not create bad habits.

8th. Such as will not interfere with duties of home or school.

986. Give such games or plays as are approved or disapproved above, and your reason why.

987. *With whom* should children play?

1st. With such playmates as our parents prefer.

2d. With such as have good characters.

3d. With such as we know have good habits.

988. Give the reason for the above three answers.

989. *How* should children play?

1st. So that others shall enjoy our company.

2d. Always in good temper.

3d. Always with kindness and politeness.

PRACTICAL JOKES.

990. What is a practical joke?

It is a deception practised upon another in order to make him the subject of ridicule.

991. Why are practical jokes always harmful?

1st. They are the result of deception.

2d. They are always rude and offensive.

A Silly Practical Joke.

A young woman about twenty-eight years of age, daughter of a prominent man on Staten Island, visited a New York dentist not long since and had some teeth extracted after taking laughing-gas. She then determined to have some fun with the folks at home by telegraphing that she was dead. She accordingly sent a despatch to her pastor, who was preaching at the time, in observance of St. Andrew's day, that she had died from the effects of inhaling laughing-gas. The startling announcement created excitement among the congregation, the young lady being well known to them all. The services were at once concluded, and word was sent to her father, who hastened to the dentist's rooms. There he was surprised as well as overjoyed to ascertain that his daughter had but a short time previously started for home in excellent health. When asked by her parents what induced her to send such a despatch, she said that *she did it for fun.*

992. Relate the silly practical joke.
993. In what did the young woman's fun consist?
994. What would you call her conduct?

A Stupid Practical Joke.

The clerks in a Boston book-store had acquired a habit of playing off little tricks upon one another,—practical joking, they called it,—and one of the tricks was this: If one of the clerks chanced to see another in a stooping posture, selecting books from lower shelves, he would seize a board, perhaps part of a box-cover, and smartly spank the stooping victim.

Jerry P. was one of these clerks, a simple-minded, good-natured fellow from Vermont, always ready and willing for the hardest kind of work, and prized by his employers accordingly. Jerry had of late been the chief victim of the spanking process, and he was determined upon revenge, —not with malevolence, nor yet with indignation, but simply in the way of fair play. To this end he watched for an opportunity.

One afternoon, upon returning to the store from an errand, the longed-for opportunity seemed to present itself, and Jerry seized it instantly. At the far end of one of the long counters he saw an individual overhauling books on the very bottom shelf, his body bent at a most tempting angle. Jerry was sure it was Tom S., from whose hands he had received many an emphatic spank, and now was the time to pay off old scores. So he selected a splendid board, and creeping noiselessly to the spot, he gave the stooping man a blow that sounded through the store like the bursting of a retort, and brought him to an erect position like a jack-in-a-box.

Here was a fix. Tom S., at the sound of the blow, appeared from another part of the store, while the gentleman who had been struck stood in utter bewilderment, rubbing away at the aching part most assiduously; and poor Jerry then discovered, to his dismay and deep regret, that he had struck his employer's pastor, Rev. Dr. B., who had been curiously searching among a lot of old Greek and Hebrew books. Jerry wept with shame and confusion, and was forgiven; and from that time that particular species of amusement was discontinued in the store.

995. Relate Jerry's stupid blunder.

996. Do tears always relieve us from the effects of stupid jokes? Why?

997. Is a joke of that kind very funny after all?

A Thoughtless Practical Joke.

Mr. Prescott, the historian, lost the use of one of his eyes by rough play in college. After dinner, one day, in Commons Hall, a student, bent on having a little fun, threw a hard crust of bread. It struck young Prescott in the eye, inflicting a severe wound, from whose effects he never recovered. The nerves were so seriously injured that their tone could not be restored, and the eye was of little use for the rest of life.

Mr. Prescott, with his generous nature, cherished no feelings of resentment towards the student who had inflicted such a grievous injury. But he thought it singular that no apology was made and no regret expressed ; and every honorable mind shares his wonder. The code of college honor is often strangely perverted from virtue and justice. Collegians who think it no disgrace to be guilty of mean and unjust acts, count it very degrading to their dignity to make an apology. The offender against Mr. Prescott must have been one of this class. He had no sense of shame for the reckless act that inflicted a life-long injury.

998. Relate the thoughtless practical joke by which Mr. Prescott lost his eye.

999. Was the careless throwing of a bread-crust in a crowd of students fun? Was it fun to Prescott? Why?

1000. What should the student who did the injury have done? Why?

A Serious Practical Joke.

It takes two to make a joke, as it takes two to make a quarrel, and unless the two are *the right persons*, the joke will be likely to end in a quarrel.

The London *Pictorial World* has the following : "One day, in Regent Street, I saw a friend looking into a shop-window, and in a very tempting position. He wore a frock-coat, and his white pocket-handkerchief was just exposed. It were easy to show him how easy a pocket were picked, I said to myself, and proceeded to extract the tempting pocket-handkerchief. In the act of my amateur larceny he turned round. To my horror, I found it was not my friend! I protested I had made a mistake ; that I thought it was So-and-so, the very image of him ; that I was picking pockets for fun, and so on. He said that was all very well, but he could not be ' kidded' in that fashion. He had a duty towards society to perform. He positively gave me in charge! In a minute the horror of my position flashed across me. I saw my name in the police reports. I heard in anticipation the remarks of kind friends, ' It looks very suspicious,' and so on ; and I felt that my life would be written for the *World*. But, luckily, the police-man refused to take the charge, and ' recognize me as a pickpocket.' "

1001. Relate the story of the serious practical joke.

1002. What is meant when it is said that it takes two to make a joke?

1003. Why was the joke so serious and so hard to explain ?

The Cruel Practical Joke.

Tormenting in fun is the worst possible joking, and tor-menting in spite is the poorest kind of vengeance. The Albany (Missouri) *Ledger* says,—

" Several days since Mr. Shaul, in company with one or two other men, started to Albany in a wagon, and a dog belonging to one of the men was following, which was against the wish of the parties. So they concluded to tie a small bunch of hay to his tail, which they did, and satu-rated it with coal oil and set it on fire. The dog no sooner discovered his peril than he started to run, going between the horses, which became so frightened that they ran away. After this the dog made for home, which he reached in

less time than it takes to relate the facts connected with
his arrival.   As was natural he sought refuge in the stack-
yard, and soon, to his great satisfaction, no doubt, he saw
the flames looming up from one of the haystacks.   Mr.
Shaul and friends hastened to the scene, and made all the
efforts in their power to extinguish the flames, which they
failed to do."

1004. Relate the cruel practical joke.
1005. Should cruelty ever be enjoyed as fun?

A Fatal Practical Joke.

A letter from St. Louis to the New York *Herald* relates
how a sally of coarse jesting ended in the death of an
inoffensive young man :

"One evening, not long since, a number of young men
and boys were lounging at the corner of Jefferson Avenue
and Pacific Street, in the western part of the city, when
three men in a buggy drove past.   Something peculiar in
the style of the horse attached to the buggy caused the boys
to hoot and utter coarse jokes, whereupon the men in the
buggy pulled up, and considerable badinage followed, during which some person in the crowd crossed the reins in
the bridle of the horse.   This enraged the men in the
buggy, one of whom jumped out and demanded to know
who did it.   A young man named George Williams, aged
twenty-one, who was simply a looker-on, was pointed out
as the practical joker, and the man from the buggy attacked him, and a scuffle ensued, in which a pistol was
discharged.   Young Williams fell to the pavement and
died within three minutes."

A sadly instructive chapter on the fruits of idleness and
ill-manners.   The trouble began with *loafing ;* loafing led
to blackguarding; blackguarding brought on a quarrel ;

the quarrel ended in murder. And the victim of the murder was perhaps the only one not to blame. That the men would have done better to drive on without minding the insult, and were wrong too in carrying concealed fire-arms, does not change the responsibility.

1006. Relate the story of the fatal practical joke.

1007. Give the successive steps that led to the murder.

1008. What rule would have prevented all these practical jokes?

1009. Was the result of any of these jokes funny?

1010. Is it safe to run the risk of a practical joke? Why?

The following questions need not be answered aloud:

1011. Are your amusements such as your parents approve?

1012. Do your plays interfere with your duties at home or at school?

1013. Do you enjoy a practical joke on somebody else?

1014. Do you enjoy a practical joke when you are the victim?

1015. Do you lose your temper when at play?

1016. Do you ever cheat when you play?

PRACTICAL APPLICATION OF THE PRINCIPLES OF POLITENESS AT SCHOOL.

To the following questions pupils can give their own answers, with the reasons for their opinions:

1017. How should pupils act at school as to punctuality?

1018. Regularity in attendance? Why?

1019. Obedience to school laws?

1020. Forgetfulness of duty?

1021. Preparation of lessons?

1022. Respectful attention to the teacher?

1023. Neat and tidy appearance?

1024. Feelings toward the teacher?

1025. Feelings toward school-mates?

1026. Treatment of school-mates?

1027. Treatment of tattlers?

1028. Being witnesses?

1029. The care of our books?

1030. Abusing and defacing school property?

1031. Writing their own or others' names on or about the school?

1032. Being always polite and truthful?

1033. Defending the rights of those who are wronged?

1034. Always being a peacemaker?

1035. Always daring to be laughed at for doing right?

1036. Always fighting where fighting is a duty?

1037. Always refusing to fight when fighting would be cowardly?

One of these questions would serve as a text, with suitable illustration, for a fifteen-minutes' discussion each morning at school.

THE END.

www.ingramcontent.com/pod-product-compliance
Lightning Source LLC
Chambersburg PA
CBHW030103070426
42448CB00037B/908